THE GREAT COOKS' GUIDE TO
Pies
& Tarts

GREAT COOKS' LIBRARY

Appetizers
Breads
Cakes
Chickens, Ducks & Other Poultry
Children's Cookery
Clay Cookery
Cookies
Crêpes & Soufflés
Fish Cookery
Flambéing Desserts
Ice Cream & Other Frozen Desserts
Omelets from Around the World
Pasta & Noodle Dishes
Pies & Tarts
Rice Cookery
Salads
Soups
Vegetable Cookery
Wine Drinks
Woks, Steamers & Fire Pots

America's leading food authorities share their home-tested
recipes and expertise on cooking equipment and techniques

THE GREAT COOKS' GUIDE TO

A BEARD GLASER WOLF BOOK

RANDOM HOUSE, NEW YORK

Front Cover (left to right, top to bottom): Fresh Peach Pie, page 35 *(wooden trivet courtesy Design Research International);* Raspberry Barquettes, page 28 *(flan ring courtesy Bazaar de la Cuisine; pastry brush and marble pastry slab courtesy The Professional Kitchen).*

Back Cover (left to right, top to bottom): *(circular flan form courtesy Bazaar de la Cuisine);* Tomato-Basil Quiche, page 16 *(wooden trivet courtesy Design Research International);* Steak and Kidney Pie, page 19 *(oval stoneware pie dish courtesy La Cuisiniere).*

Interior Photographs: Page 3 (top), *flan ring courtesy Bazaar de la Cuisine;* Page 3 (bottom), *tartlet tins courtesy The Professional Kitchen;* Page 4 (top), *oval pie dish courtesy La Cuisiniere;* Page 4 (bottom), *pastry crimper courtesy H.Roth & Son; pastry brush courtesy The Professional Kitchen, pastry jagger courtesy Bazaar de la Cuisine.*

Book Design by Milton Glaser, Inc.

Cover Photograph by Richard Jeffery

Food Styling by Lucy Wing
Props selected by Yvonne McHarg and Beard Glaser Wolf Ltd.

Library of Congress Cataloguing in Publication Data
Main entry under title:

The Great Cooks' Guide to Pies & Tarts.
(The Great Cooks' Library)
1. Pastry.   I. Series.
TX773.G698   641.8'652   77-90238
ISBN: 0-394-73604-4

Manufactured in the United States of America
2 4 6 8 9 7 5 3
First Edition

We have gathered together some of the great cooks in this country to share their recipes—and their expertise—with you. As you read the recipes, you will find that in certain cases techniques will vary. This is as it should be: Cooking is a highly individual art, and our experts have arrived at their own personal methods through years of experience in the kitchen.

THE EDITORS

SENIOR EDITORS

Wendy Afton Rieder
Kate Slate

ASSOCIATE EDITORS

Lois Bloom
Susan Lipke

EDITORIAL ASSISTANT

Christopher Carter

PRODUCTION MANAGER

Emily Aronson

EDITORIAL STAFF

Mardee Haidin
Michael Sears
Patricia Thomas

CONTRIBUTORS

Eliza and Joshua Baer have worked in various phases of the restaurant business on the West Coast and are currently planning a cookbook.

Michael Batterberry, author of several books on food, art and social history, is also a painter, and is editor and food critic for a number of national magazines. He has taught at James Beard's cooking classes in New York and many of his original recipes have appeared in *House & Garden, House Beautiful* and *Harper's Bazaar.*

Paula J. Buchholz is the regional co-ordinator for the National Culinary Apprenticeship Program. She has been a food writer for the *Detroit Free Press* and for the *San Francisco Examiner.*

Vilma Liacouras Chantiles, author of *The Food of Greece*, writes a food and consumer column for the *Scarsdale* (New York) *Inquirer* and a monthly food column for the *Athenian Magazine* (Athens, Greece).

Elizabeth Schneider Colchie is a noted food consultant who has done extensive recipe development and testing as well as research into the history of foods and cookery. She was on the editorial staff of *The Cooks' Catalogue* and *The International Cooks' Catalogue* and has written numerous articles for such magazines as *Gourmet, House & Garden* and *Family Circle.*

Isabel S. Cornell, a home economist, was Associate Editor for the revised edition of *Woman's Day Encyclopedia of Cookery* and Special Projects Editor for the revised edition of *Woman's Day Collector's Cook Book.* While on the *Woman's Day* staff, she selected, tested and judged for their recipe contests.

Carol Cutler, who has been a food columnist for the *Washington Post*, is a graduate of the Cordon Bleu and L'Ecole des Trois Gourmands in Paris. She is the author of *Haute Cuisine for Your Heart's Delight* and *The Six-Minute Soufflé and Other Culinary Delights.* She has also written for *House & Garden, American Home* and *Harper's Bazaar.*

Rona Deme, a native of England, ran a pork store with her husband for 25 years and in 1972 opened up The Country Host, a gourmet food shop in New York City.

Florence Fabricant is a free-lance writer, reporting on restaurants and food for *The New York Times, New York* magazine and other publications. She was on the staff of *The Cooks' Catalogue* and editor of the paperback edition. She also contributed to *The International Cooks' Catalogue* and *Where to Eat in America.*

Emanuel and Madeline Greenberg co-authored *Whiskey in the Kitchen* and are consultants to the food and beverage industry. Emanuel, a home economist, is a regular contributor to the food columns of *Playboy* magazine. Both contribute to *House Beautiful, Harper's Bazaar* and *Travel & Leisure.*

Mireille Johnston, the author of *The Cuisine of the Sun*, a cookbook of Provençal specialties, is currently completing a book on the cooking of Burgundy, *The Cuisine of the Rose.*

Alma Lach holds a Diplôme de Cordon Bleu from Paris and has served as food editor for the *Chicago Sun-Times.* She is author of *How's and Why's of French Cooking* and *Cooking à la Cordon Bleu* as well as many other cookbooks and articles on food. She directs the Alma Lach Cooking School in Chicago and is currently the television chef on the P.B.S. program "Over Easy."

Jeanne Lesem, Family Editor of United Press International, is the author of *The Pleasures of Preserving and Pickling.*

Susan Lipke is an Associate Editor of the Great Cooks' Library series as well as *The International Cooks' Catalogue* and *The Cooks' Catalogue*, and writes and tests recipes.

Nan Mabon, a freelance food writer and cooking teacher in New York City, is also the cook for a private executive dining room on Wall Street. She studied at the Cordon Bleu in London.

Maurice Moore-Betty, owner-operator of The Civilized Art Cooking School, food consultant and restaurateur, is author of *Cooking for Occasions, The Maurice Moore-Betty Cooking School Book of Fine Cooking* and *The Civilized Art of Salad Making.*

Jane Moulton, a food writer for the *Plain Dealer* in Cleveland, took her degree in foods and nutrition. As well as reporting on culinary matters and reviewing food-related books for the *Plain Dealer*, she has worked in recipe development, public relations and catering.

Paul Rubinstein is the author of *Feasts for Two, The Night Before Cookbook* and *Feasts for Twelve (or More)*. He is a stockbroker and son of pianist Artur Rubinstein.

Maria Luisa Scott and Jack Denton Scott co-authored the popular *Complete Book of Pasta* and have also written many other books on food, including *Informal Dinners for Easy Entertaining, Mastering Microwave Cooking, The Best of the Pacific Cookbook,* and *Cook Like a Peasant, Eat Like a King.* With the renowned chef Antoine Gilly, they wrote *Feast of France.*

Satish Sehgal is the founder of the successful Indian Oven restaurant in New York City, which specializes in northern Indian cuisine. He began developing recipes for northern specialties while an engineering student in southern India and later abandoned engineering for the food world.

Raymond Sokolov, author of *The Saucier's Apprentice,* is a freelance writer with a particular interest in food.

Marion Lear Swaybill, a field producer-writer in the documentary division of NBC News in New York, long ago took up cooking as a serious avocation and has become an expert cook and baker.

Paula Wolfert, author of *Mediterranean Cooking* and *Couscous and Other Good Food from Morocco,* is also a cooking teacher and consultant. She has written articles for *Vogue* and other magazines.

Nicola Zanghi is the owner-chef of Restaurant Zanghi in Glen Cove, New York. He started his apprenticeship under his father at the age of thirteen, and is a graduate of two culinary colleges. He has been an instructor at the Cordon Bleu school in New York City.

Contents

Introduction _____1

SAVORY PIES AND TARTS

Apple, Swiss Chard and Pine Nut Pie _____10
Turkey Pot Pie _____11
Pork Pie _____12
Bisteeya _____13
Meat Loaf Strudel _____14
Onion Tart _____15
Tomato-Basil Quiche_____16
Herb and Cheese Filo Pie _____17
Leek Quiche _____18
Steak and Kidney Pie _____19
Kipper or Finnan Haddie Quiche _____20
Quiche Lorraine_____21
Spinach Quiche _____22
Clam Pie _____23
Little Pizzas_____24
Crab Quiche _____25

SWEET PIES AND TARTS

Deep-Dish Blackberry and Apple Pie_____26
Currant Tart_____27
Raspberry Barquettes _____28
Green Tomato Pie _____29
Ricotta Pie _____30
Rhubarb-Strawberry Tart _____31
Spicy Pumpkin Nut Pie _____32
Chocolate Mousse Pie _____33
Dried Apricot Tartlets _____34
Fresh Peach Pie_____35
Pecan Pie _____36
Hot Apple Tarts with Crème Frâiche _____37
Orange Tart_____38
Latticed Blueberry Pie with Almond Crust _____40

Lemon Tart _____41
Cherry Cobbler _____42
Bosc Pear Pie_____43
Maple Walnut Pie _____44
Fudge Bottom Pie _____44
Currant Chiffon Pie _____45
Mincemeat Tarts _____46
Pure Strawberry Pie _____47

SAVORY AND SWEET TURNOVERS

Turnovers Stuffed with Peas and Potatoes _____48
Fried Peach Pies _____49
Baked Savory Cheese Turnovers _____50
Fresh Blackberry Turnovers _____51
Cornish Pasties _____52
Peruvian Meat Turnovers_____53

Pies & Tarts

Pies and tarts, what tempting, tantalizing, delectable visions the words conjure for each of us! And how different the images are: cherry, with a golden lattice silhouetted in crimson; lime chiffon, cool and elegant on a palette of toasted coconut; crab quiche in a tender shell of barest brown; deep chocolate encased in mysterious spice. The mind boggles at choosing among them, and the imagination is challenged by the endless combinations possible.

Pie may be broadly defined as a food consisting of a crust and filling in complementary combination—a challenging broad base from which to create the hors d'oeuvre, entrée, and dessert temptations that we have in mind. Pies and tarts lay claim to an impressive family tree, for pastry-making can be traced as far back as the Golden Age of Greece. Visiting Romans recognized a good thing when they saw it and took the idea home with them, from whence it moved to Gaul.

The French—never ones to shirk a culinary challenge—fashioned their crust-filling inspirations into savory showcases for the delectable offerings of the provinces, and the results emerged from primitive ovens across the land as tarts, flans, quiches, and *pissaladières* (the French relative of the pizza).

From France it was as easy as pie to cross the Channel to medieval England where these new creations were well received, and it was there that pies and tarts really came into their own. The flour and water paste used for crust was not originally intended for eating; rather, it was simply an ingenious means of sealing in the juices of cooked food. Crusts absorb juices, however, and cooks nibble, so it wasn't long before a clever baker discovered that those baked pastes could be flavorful as well as practical. The result was a pastry lid for nearly every dish that graced the table, and pastry sculpture soon become the rage. The chef-artists suddenly found themselves in courtly demand, with bids for cunning creations such as "venison patties in the shape of gilded lions, pies in the form of...eagles, pasties of pheasant that seemed alive..."

In Elizabethan times, Simple Simon could well have met many a pie-man on his way to the fair, each proudly bringing the pie most favored in his county, be it squab from Cornwall or mutton from Oxford, both of which vied for high position in pie fame. Cornwall, in fact, was the heart of pie country, to the extent that "the devil himself wouldn't enter Cornwall for fear of being shut in a pie and eaten;" so it is fitting that from Cornwall came the pasty, that clever and convenient turnover, which encased an entire lunch, with a meat filling in one end and a sweet dessert in the other.

When the British came to the New World a knowledge of pies and tarts came with them, and although pies are still associated especially with New England, they moved westward with the pioneers. Soon regional pies were developed, again according to the customs and foods of the people that settled a particular area. Thus pecan pies became associated with the South, as did cream pies with the Midwest, blueberry and cherry with Michigan, and apple with the Pacific Northwest. A North Carolinian recorded, however, that he knew of only three kinds: "kivered, unkivered, and barred."

Fruit pies were the favorites, but pies of all varieties soon became the mainstay of church suppers and community gatherings. Baking competition among the ladies was often fierce, and more than one beau was won on little more than the strength of a fine pumpkin pie. In the West, the chuck wagon, where all ranch food was "dished out," became known as the pie box—in honor of the cowhands' favorite food. Americans, in effect, revere pie like the Fourth of July. They have adopted it, cherished it, coddled it, and improved and perfected it without ever letting it be long absent from their tables.

Pies and Tarts Defined. A pie is a slope-sided savory or sweet-filled pastry that is frequently encased by both a bottom and top crust. It is served directly from its baking pan or dish. Tarts, flans and quiches, on the other hand, are straight-sided and open-faced. (The terms "tart" and "flan" may be used interchangeably, although a flan more often has a filling made with custard.) Tarts are always sweet, flans can be sweet or savory, but both are traditionally baked inside a metal ring, or a square or rectangular form which is set directly on a baking sheet. The baking form is simply lifted off before serving because the pastry is firm enough to stand on its own. Tartlets, diminutive tarts, however, are commonly baked in small tins. Typically, the top of a tart or tartlet is glazed.

Quiches are savory tarts with a custard-based filling that are served as an appetizer or main course, often from the baking dish. They, as well as tarts, may also be baked in a loose-bottomed metal pan.

Although there are many variations on pastry, pie dough tends to be flaky and very tender when baked, whereas tart pastry, such as the French *pâte brisée*, is very buttery, or short, and somewhat crisp. Other European tart doughs frequently incorporate both raw and hard-cooked egg yolks for an even richer consistency that holds up well with a filling. For extra elegance, some tarts are made with puff pastry, cleverly created by folding butter into dough so that the butter and pastry form alternating layers. This causes the dough to separate, or puff up, during baking, giving the pastry a wonderfully airy, crisp texture.

Ingredients. Pies and tarts begin with crust, regardless of where it lies in relation to the filling; and although pie crust is most frequently pastry, it need by no means be limited to flour, shortening, water and seasoning.

2

Quiche and tart molds. A pretty porcelain tart dish goes easily from oven to table, but quiches and tarts may also be served free-standing by using either a pan with a loose bottom, or a flan ring on a baking sheet. The black steel of the quiche pan absorbs heat for an evenly browned crust.

Tartlet cutters and tins. These tinned-steel cutters leave scalloped edges on rounds and ovals to be pressed into tartlet pans and loaded with sweet or savory fillings either before or after baking. Cutters and tins are available in many plain or fluted sizes.

Pie plate, pie bird and deep pie dish. Here are three aids to pie-baking: a shallow pie plate made of a clay that bakes a crisp crust; an oval deep pie dish with a wide rim to hold in juices; and a ceramic pie bird that sits in the vent of a top crust to let off steam, preventing the crust from splitting and becoming soggy.

Pastry brush and wheels. Hog or nylon bristles make good pastry brushes for buttering pans and painting an egg wash or a jam glaze on crust. To cut lattice strips without tearing the dough, use a jagger with a metal wheel (bottom). The crimper (top) will quickly put a finished edge on a pie.

It can be baked with rice, potato, rye, or whole-wheat flour (for starters) and can be varied by additions of cheese, herbs and spices, yogurt, and egg yolks or whole eggs. Delicious pie crusts may also be made of graham crackers, zwieback, cookies (especially ginger snap and chocolate and vanilla wafers), cereal, coconut, biscuits, rolls, meringue, nuts, pretzels, or corn chips, usually by binding the crumbs with butter and pressing them into a buttered pan. Some of the most tempting pies and tarts are the direct result of an unusual crust and filling combination.

For the moment, however, we shall proceed with some tips and cautions regarding the pastry shell that is the bottom line for most pies. The shell begins with flour, shortening, water, and seasoning. As in any other kind of cooking, the finished product is only as good as its components, so one should use only the finest ingredients available. In most recipes, "flour" generally refers to all-purpose flour, and "butter" should be unsalted because it has the best flavor. Ice water should really be icy, not merely cold tap water, to keep the shortening cold so it will be broken into minute particles and not be merely mashed or melted. "Eggs" usually means "large" (two-ounce) eggs and "baking powder" indicates double-acting baking powder.

Equipment. Proper equipment, too, is vital before pie or tart baking even begins. The basics should include bowls of various sizes, measuring spoons and measuring cups (both the easy-to-level metal ones for dry ingredients and the less-likely-to-spill glass ones for liquids). To make extremely accurate measurements, and to follow foreign recipes, a kitchen scale is also indispenable. Once the actual preparation of a pie is under way, a pastry blender or a food processor is an excellent aid for quickly cutting shortening into flour without overworking it.

When it comes to rolling out the dough, a good heavy pin is essential, either with or without ball bearings. A pin with ball bearings requires less strength to roll out large amounts of dough, but it should be held by the roller if used to lift rolled-out dough into a baking tin so the dough doesn't slip. As for the work surface itself, nothing beats marble. Its smooth coolness makes dough decidedly easier to handle. But marble is expensive and not widely available, so an ample pastry board is a good second choice. If the dough is properly chilled no pastry cloth is required, but both pin and board should be lightly floured before they are used. On any smooth surface, a broad-bladed pastry scraper is always an asset when baking pastry and is strongly advised for quick handling of dough and a speedy clean up. A pastry crimper gives a professional-looking edge to pastry; and a soft-bristle or goose-feather pastry brush is necessary for applying glazes or washes.

For baking, non-shiny black tins and baking sheets are best because they hold rather than reflect heat and will thus bake more evenly. Quiches and tarts require a flan form or loose-bottomed pan from which they can be easily extricated. Pies are best made in metal tins, but glass pie plates are fine, too, if you remember to reduce the heat specified in a recipe by 25 F. to avoid toughening the crust.

Step By Step to a Hand-Blended Pastry Shell. Pastrymaking is wonderfully simple; but there are some pitfalls that can be most easily avoided by first mapping out the goal for most pies and tarts: A tender, flaky, golden crust, composed of flat flakes (not crumbs or beads) of pastry.

The first step is an accurate measurement of all ingredients. Then comes a thorough blending of the dry ingredients with the cold shortening. The object is to cut the shortening into fine particles, each surrounded by flour, rather than to mash or stir it in. This way the mixture will contain the maximum amount of air to make a light crust. It also serves a second function. By blending the flour and shortening thoroughly, the fat will be completely absorbed by the flour. Thus, when water or another liquid is added, it will not be able to "grab" the flour and cause the gluten in the flour to develop too fast, resulting in tough pastry. Insufficient blending of the flour and the fat may also make it necessary to add an excessive amount of water, and this, too, results in tough pastry. Overblending *after* the water is added causes the dough to become too solid, again leading to toughness. Crumbly pastry, on the other hand, is a sign of too much or too little shortening. Dough should be quickly and deftly handled, always with a light touch. It is properly blended when it pulls away cleanly from the sides of the bowl and forms a ball.

Once the dough is blended, it should be refrigerated, covered with plastic wrap for at least a half hour. (If you're pressed for time, it can be put in the freezer for 10 to 15 minutes.) Chilling helps to tenderize the dough, keeps it from shrinking during baking because it allows the gluten in the flour to relax, and makes it easier to handle. The dough should be exactly the right consistency so it has to be rolled out only *once*. Anything more constitutes overworking—of both you and it.

Blending Dough in a Food Processor. By keeping in mind only a few cautions, dough blended in a food processor is almost infallible, though some bakers will swear by the personal touch method. First, the best results are achieved when the ingredients are blended for only one crust at a time; so if you are making pastry for a two-crust pie—unless it is a very small pie—divide the recipe in half and blend the dough for the top and bottom crusts separately. Second, spin the dry ingredients and the shortening for only a few seconds, then turn off the machine and check the texture of the mixture. Repeat turning the machine on and off quickly until the ingredients resemble cornmeal. Sprinkle a little ice water over the mixture, turn on the machine, and process the dough for a few seconds more, or until it just *begins* to pull away from the sides of the container. Don't let it form a ball. Turn off the machine and scrape the dough into a ball with a rubber scraper. This method avoids overblending. Refrigerate in plastic wrap for at least half an hour.

Rolling Out the Dough. Place the dough on a lightly floured, smooth surface. Shape it into a flat disk with your hands, pushing together and closing any cracks around the edges. Sprinkle the rolling pin with flour. Beginning in the middle of the disk, roll the dough firmly but evenly away from you. Next roll from the middle toward you. Continue lifting the pin and rolling from the center outward, in all directions, working from one side to the other and taking care not to stretch the dough by attempting to roll it too thin. (Stretched dough will shrink when it is baked.) Sprinkle the rolling pin with flour if necessary to keep it from sticking and pinch closed any cracks in the edges of the dough as you roll. When ready, the dough should be about $1/8$'' thick and at least 3'' larger in diameter than the tin in which it is to fit.

Now roll half the dough around the rolling pin, picking it up with a spatula dipped in flour, if necessary. Gently lift it over the tin and unroll it into position. Press the dough into place and trim the edges about 1'' beyond the rim of the tin. Fold under the overhang, then crimp or press the rim into a decorative edge.

For a straight-sided tart or flan, let the edges of the dough fall over the sides of the pan and trim them off by rolling a pastry pin firmly across the top of the pan. (The trimmings, as with any other pie trimmings, may be rerolled and used for tartlets or lattice strips; or they may be cut into various shapes, sprinkled with cinnamon-sugar and baked for 10 to 15 minutes to make cookies.)

If the dough is made with vegetable oil instead of shortening, roll it out between two sheets of waxed paper to the desired size, lifting the paper occasionally to let the dough spread. Peel off the top piece of paper, lay the pie upside-down over the center of the dough, invert the dough and pan together, and then peel off the second sheet of paper. Proceed as for any other type of dough to trim and crimp the edges.

If the recipe calls for a baked shell, pinch the bottom of the shell when the dough is in place. This prevents air bubbles from forming while the dough is baking. Do not prick the bottom if an unbaked shell is required. In either case, refrigerate the shell for half an hour before continuing the recipe.

Baking the Shell. It is worthwhile to bake most pie and tart shells at least slightly before adding the filling. If a recipe calls for an unbaked shell, brush the shell with beaten egg white and set it in a preheated 450 F. oven for 1 or 2 minutes to bake on the glaze. This will seal the dough against the moisture of the filling, and prevent the shell from becoming soggy. Once the shell is cool, it can be filled and "kivered" or "barred" (latticed) and then baked.

Baking a pie shell "blind," means baking the dough to a pale gold before the filling is added. This is advantageous for almost all pie and tart pastry to keep it crisp. To bake a shell blind, line the pricked shell with waxed paper or foil and fill it with raw rice, dried beans or peas, the packaged aluminum pie nuggets that are now on the market for just this purpose, or any other weight that will prevent air bubbles from pushing the dough up and cracking it. (Any of these weights may be kept in a special container and reused many times.) Set the shell on a non-shiny baking sheet and bake it in a preheated 400 F. for about 10 to 15 minutes, or until the dough is just set. Remove the paper or foil with the weights and return the shell to the oven for about 10 minutes, or until it is golden. Then transfer the tin to a rack and let it cool.

Pie Fillings. Pie fillings vary so greatly that it is difficult to speak of them in a general way. Nonetheless, a few thoughts should be borne in mind.

Cobblers and deep-dish pies with their single crust may be somewhat less intimidating for a beginning baker. But they require double the amount of filling for a standard 9'' pie, or about 6 to 8 cups.

Chiffon pies are usually based on gelatin to which whole eggs or egg whites have been added, but they may also be soft custard pies lightened with whipped cream or egg whites. If making a custard filling, be sure to stir it until it is cool so that steam will not condense in it and thin it.

Fruit pies are usually thickened with flour, cornstarch or arrowroot, tapioca or custard. Because acid fruits, such as strawberries or peaches, tend to neutralize the effects of flour, it is best to use only the other thickeners with those pies. When using cornstarch or arrowroot, first dissolve it in a little of the fruit juice or water before mixing it into the fruit. Let tapioca or cornstarch sit for about 10 or 15 minutes after it has been mixed with the fruit, before it is poured into the pie shell.

Atop the Filling. As soon as a pie is filled, the top crust, if any, should be quickly rolled (as for the bottom crust) and attached. Trim the top crust even with the rim of the shell, brush the rim of the shell with water and then crimp the two edges together decoratively, with the fingers or with any of the countless narrow objects that will make an attractive edge (spoon handles, a fork, pie crimper, seashells).

Then, to prevent an unwelcome explosion, a covered pie must have some sort of escape hatch for the steam and/or bubbling juices of the filling. This is solved by cutting a vent in the dough with a knife, or by inserting a large funnel-shaped pastry tip or, more charming, a pie bird through a vent in the center of the top round of dough. A vent alone allows the juices to spill out over the crust, which, in its tantalizing way, is appealing; but a funnel tip or pie bird also contains the overflowing juices until they can settle back into the pie as it cools. The latter provide, in addition, a means of adding liquid, such as brandy, to a baked pie, if desired.

Baking. When ready for baking, a pie should be placed immediately—on a level shelf in the center of a preheated oven, giving the filling no extra time to permeate the bottom crust and make it soggy. Some pies are enhanced by a glaze, which can be melted butter; a sprinkling of sugar; a wash of milk or cream; or beaten egg, egg yolk, or egg white thinned with water. Glazes, with the exception of sugar, are brushed on with a pastry brush just before the pie goes in the oven.

Tartlets and Turnovers. Almost any pie or quiche recipe can be applied to tartlets, bearing in mind that tartlets will be baked for a considerably shorter time. Tartlet shells can be baked in small tins or in muffin or custard cups. If the dough is placed *in* the form(s), it will require foil and weights in the baking process, but the dough can also be pressed over the back(s) of the inverted form(s) to eliminate the extra step of weighting it.

Turnovers can be made with almost any pie dough and with many fillings, although there are pie fillings that for obvious reasons are inappropriate. To make turnovers, the dough is cut into rounds, squares, or rectangles of the desired size, the filling is mounded on one side of each piece, and the dough is brushed around the edges with water. It is then folded into half circles, triangles, or other shapes and the edges are crimped together firmly. Turnovers may be glazed with an egg wash or sprinkled with sugar, and then baked on a baking sheet. Some can also be deep-fried, in which case any glaze is omitted: The turnovers are lowered into several inches of hot (375 F.) oil, fried for about 3 minutes, and then transferred to paper towels to drain. For fried sweet pies, confectioners' sugar makes an appealing topping.

Freezing. Pies may be frozen either baked or unbaked, but the best results are usually obtained by freezing the unbaked shell and filling separately. Dough freezes beautifully, whether unrolled or fitted into tins; but it shouldn't be frozen for more than two months, and it should be well wrapped or covered with foil. Our pie-baking ancestors in New England froze their pies outdoors in winter, but many a pie was no doubt ruined by an unexpected thaw. Fortunately we have better methods today. Pie shells stack neatly (out of their tins) after they are frozen, so it's possible to keep a stock of several kinds and sizes in very little space. They should, however, be labeled as to whether they are sweet dessert shells or salty or flavored hors d'oeuvre and entrée shells.

To bake a frozen shell, put it in a tin and pop it directly into a preheated 425 F. oven for about 15 minutes. Many cooks feel that freezing filled pies is not entirely successful; although certain kinds, including most fruit pies and those with dense fillings, such as mincemeat, lose none of their texture or flavor to a short stint in the freezer. They are best frozen for no more than two months, however. Don't even consider freezing custard and cream pies. And if you do freeze fruit pies with fillings that have tapioca or cornstarch, increase the amount of those ingredients about 1½ times.

Freeze any filled pie before wrapping it. When ready to bake a filled frozen pie unwrap it, cut vent holes, if necessary, and place the frozen pie in the bottom rack of a preheated 450 F. oven. Bake for about 15 minutes and then reduce the heat to 375 F. and continue baking until the pie is done, about 45 or 50 minutes longer.

Final Thoughts. As you slide your masterpiece into the oven, rest assured that the splendid creation is likely to be more than well received. If there are any doubts about its being a triumph, you might bear in mind a *New York Times* editorial of 1902 that stated: "Pie is the American synonym for prosperity, and its varying contents the calendar of the changing seasons. Pie is the food of the heroic. No pie-eating people can ever be permanently vanquished." Perhaps not everyone takes pies so seriously, but that opinion epitomized the regard of Americans for one of their most beloved foods.

Savory Pies and Tarts

APPLE, SWISS CHARD AND PINE NUT PIE
(TOURTE DE BLETTES)

Mireille Johnston

8 servings

Pastry:
3 CUPS UNBLEACHED FLOUR
2 EGGS, BEATEN
½ POUND (2 STICKS) UNSALTED
  BUTTER, SOFTENED
½ CUP SUGAR
1 TABLESPOON SALT

Filling:
5 LARGE SWISS CHARD LEAVES
  (REMOVE THE WHITE STALKS AND
  KEEP FOR ANOTHER USE)*
4 LARGE GOLDEN DELICIOUS OR
  GRANNY SMITH APPLES

3 TABLESPOONS RAISINS
2 TABLESPOONS DARK RUM
4 TABLESPOONS PINE NUTS
½ CUP PLUS 3 TABLESPOONS CON-
  FECTIONERS' SUGAR
½ POUND BLAND CHEESE, SUCH AS
  GOUDA OR MILD CHEDDAR, DICED
2 EGGS, BEATEN
GRATED RIND OF 1 LEMON
2 TABLESPOONS CURRANT JELLY

1. Working quickly with the tips of the fingers, mix all the pastry ingredients to-gether on a well floured board. Pound and stretch the dough away from you with the heel of the hand to insure that all of the ingredients are well blended. Shape the dough into a ball, cover with a clean cloth and leave for 2 hours at room temperature.

2. Blanch the chard leaves in a large pot of boiling water for 4 minutes. Drain and allow to cool, then squeeze by hand to extract as much moisture as possible. Chop finely in a blender, food processor or with a knife.

3. Peel two of the apples and cut them into cubes.

4. In a saucepan, combine the raisins and rum, bring to a boil and cook for 2 minutes.

5. Preheat the oven to 375 F.

6. In a large bowl, combine the blanched Swiss chard, apple cubes, raisin mix-ture, pine nuts, ½ cup of the confectioners' sugar, cheese, eggs and lemon rind.

7. Peel the remaining two apples and cut them into slices.

8. Divide the pastry into two parts, one equal to about one-third of the dough, the other double that amount. Roll each piece of pastry as thin as possible.

9. Butter a deep, 10'' pie plate or tart mold and fit the larger circle of dough into the dish, molding it to fit the bottom and sides. Prick it all over with a fork. Spread the currant jelly over the bottom and add the filling.

10. Cover with the apple slices and top with the smaller circle of dough. Fit the two crusts together smoothly and cut off the excess dough. Prick the top crust with a fork. Bake for 30 minutes, or until golden.

11. Remove from the oven and sprinkle with the remaining 3 tablespoons of confectioners' sugar.

* If you cannot find Swiss chard in your neighborhood, replace the 5 large leaves of Swiss chard with 1 cup of cooked and thoroughly drained, chopped spinach (two 10-ounce packages of frozen chopped spinach or 2 pounds of fresh spinach) and proceed as above.

TURKEY POT PIE

Paul Rubinstein

6 servings

1 WHOLE TURKEY BREAST (ABOUT 4 TO 5 POUNDS)
1 CUP SLICED CELERY
1 LARGE ONION, PEELED
4 CARROTS, SCRAPED AND SLICED INTO 1''-LONG PIECES
1 BAY LEAF
1 TABLESPOON SALT
24 SMALL, WHOLE WHITE ONIONS, PEELED
24 SMALL TO MEDIUM-SIZED FRESH WHITE MUSHROOMS

5 TABLESPOONS BUTTER
2 CUPS FLOUR, APPROXIMATELY
3 CUPS CHICKEN BROTH OR CHICKEN BOUILLON
¼ TEASPOON FRESHLY GROUND WHITE PEPPER
3 TEASPOONS DOUBLE-ACTING BAKING POWDER
2 TABLESPOONS VEGETABLE SHORTENING
⅔ CUP MILK

1. In a deep pot or stockpot, combine the turkey breast, celery, large onion, carrots, bay leaf, 2 teaspoons of the salt and enough cold water to cover the turkey. Bring to a boil, reduce the heat to a simmer, cover and simmer about 1 hour, until the turkey meat is tender. Add the small onions and the mushrooms to the pot after the first 30 minutes of cooking time.

2. Remove the turkey to a cutting board and allow it to cool.

3. Remove the cooked celery, carrots, whole small onions and mushrooms from the pot with a slotted spoon and place them in a deep, round casserole. Discard the large onion.

4. Cut away the bones and skin from the cooled turkey, and cut the meat into approximately 1'' cubes. Add the turkey cubes to the cooked vegetables in the casserole.

11

Continued from preceding page

5. Preheat the oven to 450 F.

6. In a saucepan, melt the butter and add 5 tablespoons of the flour. Blend into a paste and cook 3 minutes over medium heat, stirring. Add the chicken broth, a little at a time, forming a thick sauce, then stir in the pepper. Pour this sauce into the casserole over the turkey and vegetables and toss with two spoons.

7. Sift 1½ cups of the remaining flour with the baking powder and 1 teaspoon salt. Cut the shortening into the dry ingredients with a pastry blender or two knives, until well distributed. Add the milk, knead until a smooth and moist dough is formed. Place on a lightly floured pastry board and roll out into a circle the size of the top of the casserole.

8. Carefully place the circle of dough in the casserole over the turkey and vegetables. Slash through the dough in three or four places, making 1½"-long cuts.

9. Bake in the preheated oven for 25 minutes, until the crust is golden brown and puffed.

10. Serve directly from the casserole at the table, cutting wedges of crust, then spooning the filling on top. Serve with rice. No other vegetables are needed.

PORK PIE

Jane Moulton

One 9" pie

2 POUNDS GROUND LEAN PORK
1⅓ CUPS COARSELY CHOPPED ONION
⅓ CUP FINELY CHOPPED GREEN
  PEPPER
2 TEASPOONS SALT
½ TEASPOON PEPPER (OPTIONAL)

1 TEASPOON POULTRY SEASONING
1 TEASPOON DRIED SAVORY
1 CUP SOUR CREAM
3 TABLESPOONS ALL-PURPOSE FLOUR
PASTRY FOR A 9", DOUBLE-CRUST PIE

1. In a large skillet, brown the pork over medium heat, stirring frequently. When it begins to brown, add the onion and green pepper. Reduce the heat and continue to cook the meat until all traces of pink color disappear, about 20 minutes longer.

2. Drain the fat from the skillet. Add the salt, pepper (if desired), poultry seasoning and savory to the pork and mix well.

3. Combine the sour cream and flour and blend well. Add this to the meat mixture and mix well.

4. Preheat the oven to 425 F.

5. Line a 9" pie pan with the rolled out pastry and fill it with the meat mixture. Apply the top crust, flute the edge and cut steam vents in the top.

6. Bake in the preheated oven for 13 minutes, or until the crust just begins to brown. Reduce the heat to 375 F. and continue baking until the crust is golden brown, about 30 minutes longer.

BISTEEYA

Paula Wolfert

12 servings

4 POUNDS SQUABS OR CHICKEN LEGS AND THIGHS, PLUS GIBLETS
1 CUP CHOPPED FRESH PARSLEY, MIXED WITH SOME CHOPPED FRESH CORIANDER
1 LARGE ONION, GRATED
¼ TEASPOON TURMERIC
SEVERAL PINCHES OF PULVERIZED SAFFRON
1 SCANT TEASPOON FRESHLY GROUND BLACK PEPPER
¾ TEASPOON GROUND GINGER
THREE 3"-LONG STICKS CINNAMON
½ POUND (2 STICKS) UNSALTED BUTTER
SALT
3 CUPS WATER
1 POUND WHOLE BLANCHED ALMONDS
¼ CUP SALAD OIL
CONFECTIONERS' SUGAR
GROUND CINNAMON
¼ CUP LEMON JUICE
10 EGGS, WELL BEATEN
½ TO ¾ POUND *FILO* OR STRUDEL PASTRY LEAVES

1. Put the squabs (or chicken legs and thighs) in a large casserole with the giblets, fresh mixed herbs, onion, spices, half the butter, a little salt and the water. Bring to a boil, cover and simmer for 1 hour.

2. Meanwhile, brown the almonds lightly in the salad oil. Drain, cool and crush with a rolling pin until coarsely ground. Combine with ⅓ cup confectioners' sugar and 1½ teaspoons cinnamon. Set aside.

3. Remove the poultry, giblets, cinnamon sticks and any loose bones from the casserole and set aside.

4. Reduce the remaining liquid to 1¾ cups by rapid boiling. Lower the heat to a simmer and add the lemon juice.

5. Pour the beaten eggs into the simmering sauce and stir constantly until the eggs cook and congeal. They should become curdy but not too dry. Transfer the eggs to a colander and let drain. Salt to taste.

6. Shred the poultry into 1½" pieces and chop the giblets. Discard the bones and cinnamon sticks.

7. Clarify the remaining stick of butter and set it aside.

8. Preheat the oven to 425 F.

9. Brush the cake, pizza or *paella* pan with some of the clarified butter. Cover the bottom of the pan with a leaf of pastry. Drape several more pastry leaves (each brushed on the top with butter) one at a time into the pan. One half of each of the leaves should extend beyond the pan sides; the other half should cover the bottom of the pan. Arrange the leaves in such a way that the entire bottom is covered.

10. Place the chunks of poultry and giblets around the edges of the pastry-lined pan, then work toward the center. Cover this layer with the well-drained egg mixture; then sprinkle with the almond-sugar mixture.

11. Cover the layers with all but 2 of the remaining pastry leaves, brushing each very lightly with butter. Fold the extended pastry leaves over the top of the pie to cover and enclose it. Place the remaining 2 leaves over the top, lightly

Continued from preceding page

buttering each, and tucking them under neatly around the edges. Pour any remaining butter around the edge.

12. Bake for 10 minutes in the preheated oven. Shake the pan to loosen the pie and run a spatula around the edges. Pour off the excess butter. Invert on a large platter, return to the pan and continue baking for another 10 minutes.

13. Remove, dust the top with confectioners' sugar and run crisscrossing lines of cinnamon over the top. Serve very hot.

MEAT LOAF STRUDEL

Isabel S. Cornell

6 servings

2 EGGS
1 TEASPOON SALT
¼ TEASPOON FRESHLY GROUND
  BLACK PEPPER
½ TEASPOON DRIED OREGANO
2 TABLESPOONS MINCED SHALLOTS
½ CLOVE GARLIC, PEELED AND
  PRESSED
¼ CUP LIGHT CREAM
FINE, DRY BREAD CRUMBS

1 POUND GROUND MEAT LOAF MIX
  (⅓ EACH PORK, BEEF AND LAMB
  OR VEAL)
½ CUP CHOPPED, COOKED MUSH-
  ROOMS
⅓ CUP SHREDDED SWISS CHEESE
4 SHEETS (ABOUT 17" x 23" EACH)
  STRUDEL LEAVES OR *FILO* DOUGH
MELTED BUTTER
PAPRIKA

1. Preheat the oven to 375 F.

2. With a fork, thoroughly mix the eggs, salt, pepper, oregano, shallots, garlic, cream and ¼ cup of bread crumbs.

3. Beat in the ground meat, mushrooms and cheese. Set aside.

4. On a barely damp towel (not wet), carefully spread out one sheet of strudel or *filo* dough; brush it gently with melted butter and sprinkle very lightly with fine bread crumbs. Spread another sheet of dough carefully on top of the first, brush with butter and sprinkle with crumbs.

   Note: The packaged dough leaves are very delicate and need careful handling. Keep them covered when not using. When they dry out they will crack, and if they get wet spots they will tear.

5. Shape the meat mixture into a cylinder and set it across one narrow end of the pastry sheets, leaving a ¾" margin of the dough free at each end of the meat roll. Gently pick up the corners of the towel at the meat end and use it to roll the meat in the prepared sheets of dough; fold in the ends of the dough. Make the final turn of the roll onto a sheet of waxed paper for easy lifting.

6. Lay a third sheet of dough on the towel, brush it with melted butter and sprinkle with bread crumbs; place the last sheet of dough on top, butter it and sprinkle with crumbs.

7. Set the encased meat roll across one of the narrow ends of the dough, pick up

the ends of the towel and roll it up in the prepared leaves and onto a large, greased pan with sides. Set the roll seam-side down and fold the ends in as best you can. Brush the top with melted butter and sprinkle with paprika.

8. Bake in the preheated oven for about 1 hour, or until the filling is done and the top is a delicate brown.

9. Remove the strudel from the oven and let it stand about 5 minutes to set. Cut it diagonally for serving. The strudel is good hot or cold, and can be frozen either before or after baking. Sour cream seasoned with sliced scallions or chives, a little mustard, salt and pepper is a good accompaniment.

ONION TART (PISSALADIÈRE)

Mireille Johnston

6 servings

Onion Purée:
12 MEDIUM-SIZED YELLOW ONIONS
  (ABOUT 3 POUNDS)
2 TABLESPOONS OLIVE OIL
2 CLOVES GARLIC, PEELED AND
  CRUSHED
1 BAY LEAF
1 TEASPOON THYME
FRESHLY GROUND BLACK PEPPER
½ TEASPOON SALT

Crust:
¼ TEASPOON ACTIVE DRY YEAST
¼ CUP LUKEWARM WATER

1 TEASPOON SALT
1 CUP UNBLEACHED FLOUR
1 TEASPOON OLIVE OIL

Garnish:
6 ANCHOVY FILLETS
1 TABLESPOON OLIVE OIL
12 TO 18 SMALL BLACK OLIVES FROM
  NICE, OR PITTED, LARGE OIL-CURED
  BLACK ONES, QUARTERED

1. To make the onion purée, peel and very finely mince the onions. A food processor makes marvelously quick work of this task.

2. In a large frying pan, warm the olive oil and add the minced onion, garlic, bay leaf, thyme, pepper and salt (the salt draws water from the onions, preventing them from turning brown).

3. Cover tightly and simmer gently over the lowest heat for 1 to 1½ hours, or until the onion has completely dissolved into a pale purée.

4. Remove the pan from the heat and squeeze the onion gently to one side of the pan with a slotted spoon, drawing off the liquid. Pour off the liquid and set it aside.

5. In a large bowl, dissolve the yeast in the water. Let it stand for 5 to 10 minutes, preferably in a warm place.

6. Stir in 1 tablespoon of reserved onion liquid, the salt and flour, and mix well.

   Note: If there is not enough onion liquid, use olive oil.

7. Knead the dough on a floured board for 20 minutes, or until it is soft and smooth.

Continued from preceding page

Place in a greased bowl and turn it over to grease the other side. Cover with a damp cloth.

8. Turn the oven to 300 F. for about 30 seconds. Put in the dough and shut off the heat. Let the dough rise there until it has doubled in bulk, about 1 hour.

9. Punch it down, sprinkle with the olive oil and knead it in the bowl for 3 minutes. Re-cover with a damp cloth and let it rise again in the oven for 10 minutes. Remove the dough.

10. Preheat the oven to 375 F.

11. Oil an 8'' x 13'' baking pan or a fluted, round French tart pan.

12. On a floured board, roll out the dough with a rolling pin, then lay it over the pan and, with your hands, stretch it along the sides of the pan so that the crust has ¾''-high sides.

13. Check the onion purée for seasoning and spoon it into the crust.

14. If a baking dish is used, arrange the anchovy fillets on top of the tart in a lattice pattern; if a tart pan is used, arrange the fillets like the spokes of a wheel.

15. Sprinkle the top with the olive oil and bake in the preheated oven for 1 hour, or until the dough has separated from the sides of the pan and is golden and crisp.

16. Remove from the oven and dot with olives. This tart tastes best warm, but reheats very well.

TOMATO-BASIL QUICHE

Susan Lipke

One 9" tart

1 POUND ONIONS, PEELED AND SLICED
3 TO 4 TABLESPOONS OLIVE OIL
1¾ POUNDS RIPE FRESH TOMATOES (PREFERABLY PLUM), PEELED, SEEDED, SQUEEZED AND CHOPPED
1½ TEASPOONS SALT
2 EGGS
½ CUP HEAVY CREAM

FRESHLY GROUND BLACK PEPPER
¾ CUP COARSELY CHOPPED, LOOSELY PACKED FRESH BASIL LEAVES
ONE 9" PASTRY SHELL, PARTIALLY BAKED
2 TO 4 TABLESPOONS GRATED PARMESAN

1. Preheat the oven to 375 F.

2. In a skillet, slowly sauté the onions in the olive oil until golden and completely soft and wilted.

3. Stir in the tomatoes and 1 teaspoon of the salt, cover and cook over low heat for 5 minutes. Remove the cover, turn up the heat and cook, stirring occasionally, until the rendered tomato juices have evaporated, at least 10 minutes. Let cool a little.

4. In a bowl, combine the eggs, cream, the remaining ½ teaspoon of salt and a liberal quantity of freshly ground black pepper. Beat together lightly, then stir in the basil and cooled onion-tomato mixture.

5. Place the pastry shell in its tin on a baking sheet and turn the filling mixture into it. Sprinkle with the Parmesan and dribble on a little olive oil.

6. Bake for 30 to 35 minutes, until slightly puffed and golden brown on top.

HERB AND CHEESE FILO PIE

Michael Batterberry

8 to 12 servings

In this delicious dish, Northern Italy's classic green-vegetable pie, *torta di verdura*, is integrated with the savory *filo* pastries of the eastern Mediterranean.

1 POUND (4 STICKS) UNSALTED BUTTER, CLARIFIED
2 TABLESPOONS OLIVE OIL
3 TABLESPOONS MINCED SHALLOTS
5 CUPS COARSELY CHOPPED, FIRMLY PACKED SWISS CHARD (LEAVES ONLY*)
½ CUP COARSELY CHOPPED SCAL-LIONS
2½ TEASPOONS KOSHER SALT
6 EGGS, LIGHTLY BEATEN
1 POUND (ABOUT 2¼ CUPS) "CREAM STYLE" COTTAGE CHEESE

2½ CUPS GRATED GRUYÈRE
1 CUP SOUR CREAM
2 CUPS FRESHLY GRATED PARMESAN
¼ TEASPOON FRESHLY GRATED NUTMEG
1½ TEASPOONS DRIED BASIL
FRESHLY GROUND BLACK PEPPER
2 CUPS COARSELY CHOPPED, FIRMLY PACKED ITALIAN PARSLEY
2 CUPS COARSELY CHOPPED FRESH DILL
1 POUND *FILO* PASTRY LEAVES

1. Preheat the oven to 400 F.

2. In a frying pan, heat 4 tablespoons of the clarified butter with the olive oil and sauté the shallots until pale gold, 3 to 4 minutes.

3. Add the Swiss chard, scallions and ½ teaspoon of the salt, tossing constantly with a wooden spoon until the chard wilts somewhat and releases some of its juices, about 3 minutes. Remove from the heat and let cool.

4. With a large fork, lightly mix and mash together the eggs, cottage cheese, Gruyère, sour cream, ¾ cup of the Parmesan, the nutmeg, basil, the 2 remaining teaspoons of salt and an assertive amount of freshly ground black pepper —at least 16 twists of the peppermill.

5. Stir the chopped parsley and dill into the cheese mixture until evenly blended. Add the chard mixture, including any juices, and blend.

6. Brush a 14" enameled cast-iron *paella* pan (or a similar large, round, shallow dish) well with the clarified butter.

7. Divide the pastry leaves into more or less equal thirds and insert strips of paper between the thirds to remind yourself when the first and second portions have been used up. Cover the leaves with a just-damp towel to keep them from drying out.

8. Place the first third of the pastry leaves as smoothly as possible in the pan,

Continued from preceding page

one at a time, in an overlapping pinwheel fashion. Brush each pastry leaf with the clarified butter before putting the next leaf down. The edges of the leaves will hang several inches over the sides of the pan, but be sure these dangling edges are well buttered.

9. When this first of three batches has been layered, spread evenly with half of the filling. Layer the next third of *filo* leaves in the same manner, then spread with the remaining filling.

10. To layer the final batch of leaves, alter your technique by crimping the overhanging edges of the leaves so that they lie within the confines of the pan's periphery—they will look rather like rumpled bottom sheets on an unmade bed. Butter each as before, sprinkling lightly with Parmesan between each layer (use ¾ cup of cheese in all).

11. Butter the final top leaves generously and fold the hanging pastry edges from the first two layers back over the top of the pie. Brush the rough seams well with the last of the butter to make them stick together as a whole.

12. Bake the pie in the preheated oven for 20 minutes.

13. Reduce the heat to 350 F., sprinkle the crust with the remaining ½ cup of Parmesan and continue baking for another 15 to 20 minutes. Do not let the pie overbrown.

14. Excellent as a main course, preceded by *prosciutto* and melon, for a late summer meal. A cooled, light red wine makes the cheeses sing, but a simple, sturdy white would also go well if that's your mood.

Note: To gild the lily, serve the pie sizzling hot with a cold sauce made of equal parts sour cream and yogurt beaten smooth with dashes of salt, Tabasco and rice vinegar, and thickened with a lavish amount of minced chives and, if you like, a handful of chopped walnuts.

* Save the stems for a variety of wok dishes.

LEEK QUICHE (FLAMICHE)

Maria Luisa Scott and Jack Denton Scott

6 servings

2 TABLESPOONS BUTTER
1 LARGE BUNCH LEEKS, THOROUGHLY
  WASHED AND CHOPPED (WHITE
  PART ONLY)
½ TEASPOON SALT, APPROXIMATELY
PEPPER
4 EGGS
1 TABLESPOON FLOUR

¼ TEASPOON DRY MUSTARD
¼ TEASPOON MACE
2 CUPS LIGHT CREAM
1 DEEP, 9" PASTRY SHELL, PARTIALLY
  BAKED
½ CUP GRATED GRUYÈRE CHEESE
6 SLICES BACON, COOKED CRISP
  AND CRUMBLED

1. Preheat the oven to 375 F.

2. In a saucepan, over medium heat, melt the butter. Add the leeks and cook, covered, until soft. Remove the cover and cook over high heat until most of the liquid has evaporated. Season with salt and pepper to taste. Set aside.

3. In a bowl, lightly beat the eggs. Mix in the flour, mustard, mace and ½ teaspoon of salt. Stir in the cream.

4. Line the bottom of the pastry shell with the leeks. Sprinkle the cheese over the leeks. Carefully pour in the egg-cream mixture.

5. Place the quiche on a cookie sheet and bake in the preheated oven for 30 minutes.

6. Sprinkle the crumbled bacon over the *flamiche* and bake 10 minutes more, or until the custard is set and the top is golden.

STEAK AND KIDNEY PIE

Rona Deme

6 to 8 servings

Pastry:
2 CUPS ALL-PURPOSE FLOUR
1 TEASPOON SALT
4 OUNCES (½ CUP) COLD LARD
4 TABLESPOONS (½ STICK) COLD
  BUTTER
¼ TO ⅓ CUP ICE WATER

Filling:
1 LARGE BEEF KIDNEY
½ CUP OIL
½ CUP LEMON JUICE
2 TABLESPOONS VINEGAR
1 TO 2 TABLESPOONS MINCED ONION
FRESHLY GROUND BLACK PEPPER
8 TABLESPOONS (1 STICK) BUTTER
2 MEDIUM-SIZED ONIONS, CHOPPED
4 POUNDS BEEF SIRLOIN, CUT INTO
  2" CUBES

FLOUR
BOUQUET GARNI (CHEESECLOTH BAG
  CONTAINING BAY LEAF, THYME AND
  SEVERAL SPRIGS PARSLEY)
1½ POUNDS CARROTS, CUT INTO
  2"-LONG PIECES
2 TABLESPOONS SALT
1 DOZEN LARGE MUSHROOMS,
  CLEANED
½ CUP FLOUR MIXED WITH ¾ CUP
  WATER TO FORM A PASTE
3 TABLESPOONS WORCESTERSHIRE
  SAUCE
1 EGG YOLK BEATEN WITH A FEW
  DROPS OF WATER

1. To make the pastry, toss the flour and salt together in a bowl. Cut in the lard and butter until the mixture is mealy, but do not overwork.

2. Add ¼ cup of the water to the flour and salt and rapidly stir the mixture with a fork until all the flour is moistened. Add more water if the pastry is too dry, but be careful not to make it sticky.

3. Gather the pastry into a ball and knead it once or twice to combine all the ingredients. Refrigerate until ready to use.

4. To make the filling, cut the kidney into small cubes and remove the suet.

5. Place the kidney in a bowl with the oil, lemon juice, vinegar, minced onion and

Continued from preceding page

pepper and marinate for 1 hour.

6. In a very large, heavy saucepan, melt the butter, add the onion and saute it lightly.

7. Dredge the sirloin cubes in flour and add them to the saucepan. Toss and mix the meat until it is sticky all over—all the flour should be coated with butter.

8. Add the kidney with its marinade to the pan along with the *bouquet garni*, the salt and enough cold water to cover the ingredients by 2''. Simmer for 1 hour.

9. Add the carrots and mushrooms to the pan and simmer for 45 minutes longer, or until the meat is tender.

10. Stir the flour/water paste, a little at a time, into the meat mixture to thicken the gravy. After all the paste has been added, simmer the meat about 5 minutes longer; then add the Worcestershire sauce and remove the meat from the heat. Let cool.

11. Preheat the oven to 350 F.

12. Turn the filling into two large (about 7- to 8-cup), deep, oval pie dishes, or four smaller, baking dishes.

13. Roll out the pastry to a thickness of ¼'' and lay it over the filling. Trim and crimp the edges.

14. Make pastry leaves with the crust trimmings. Brush the perimeter of the pie with the beaten egg yolk and arrange the leaves around it. Then brush the leaves with the egg yolk as well. Finally, cut one of several steam vents in the pastry.

15. Place the pie in the preheated oven and bake for 1 hour to 1 hour and 10 minutes, or until the crust is nicely browned and the filling is piping hot.

KIPPER OR FINNAN HADDIE QUICHE

Paula Wolfert

4 servings

8 OUNCES KIPPERS (SMOKED HER-RING) OR FINNAN HADDIES (SMOKED HADDOCK)
1 CUP HEAVY CREAM
3 EGGS
2 TABLESPOONS PREPARED HORSE-RADISH

2 TABLESPOONS CHOPPED PARSLEY
SALT
FRESHLY GROUND BLACK PEPPER
ONE 8'' PASTRY SHELL, PARTIALLY BAKED
1 TABLESPOON LEMON JUICE

1. Preheat the oven to 375 F.

2. Wrap the kippers or finnan haddies in foil and set in the oven to heat for 5 minutes.

3. Meanwhile, combine the cream, eggs, horseradish, parsley, a pinch of salt and plenty of freshly ground pepper.

4. Remove the kippers or finnan haddies from the oven (but leave the oven set at 375 F.) and add the cooking juices to the cream mixture.

5. Skin, bone and flake the fish and scatter the pieces over the bottom of the pastry shell. Sprinkle with lemon juice and pour in the cream mixture.

6. Set the pie shell on a baking sheet in the center of the preheated oven to bake for 25 to 30 minutes, or until set, puffed and golden brown. Serve hot or cold.

QUICHE LORRAINE

Alma Lach

6 to 8 servings

The crust recipe I have included with this quiche is large enough for two 8'' tart shells, because I feel the combination of these specific quantities of ingredients produces the ideal crust. It is also just as easy to make two crusts as one, and it's always handy to have extra pastry in the freezer. Consider rolling it out and placing it in a tart form before freezing; it will be ready for pre-baking or filling when you need it.

Crust (Enough for Two 8'' Shells):
2 CUPS SIFTED ALL-PURPOSE FLOUR
½ CUP SIFTED CAKE FLOUR
1 TABLESPOON CORNSTARCH
½ TEASPOON SALT
1 TEASPOON CONFECTIONERS' SUGAR
12 TABLESPOONS (1½ STICKS) BUTTER, PLIABLE BUT COOL
1 WHOLE EGG, LIGHTLY BEATEN
2 TO 3 TABLESPOONS COLD MILK, APPROXIMATELY

Filling:
2 LARGE ONIONS, THINLY SLICED
2 TABLESPOONS BUTTER
6 SLICES BACON, CUT INTO ½'' PIECES
¼ POUND GRUYÈRE OR SWISS CHEESE, THINLY SLICED
2 TEASPOONS CORNSTARCH
½ TEASPOON SALT
DASH OF PEPPER
FRESHLY GRATED NUTMEG
1 CUP HEAVY CREAM
1 CUP MILK
1 EGG YOLK

1. Sift together the all-purpose and cake flours and the cornstarch onto a marble slab or into a large mixing bowl. Make a well in the center and add the salt, sugar and butter. Blend with a pastry blender or the fingertips until the mixture is in tiny lumps. Add the egg and enough milk to make a dough. Form into a ball and place on a work surface.

2. Using the heel of your hand, push the dough away from you in little bits, then collect it into a ball and push it out again. Cover with plastic wrap and refrigerate several hours in the vegetable bin.

3. Preheat the oven to 450 F.

4. Cut the chilled dough in half and shape each half into a ball. Cover one of the balls with plastic wrap and refrigerate or freeze for future use. On a floured surface, roll out the other ball of dough to a thickness of a little more than $\frac{1}{16}$''.

5. Place the dough in an 8'' pie pan, tart shell or flan ring. Line the dough with

21

Continued from preceding page

foil; then, using an ice pick, punch some holes through the foil and dough to allow the steam to escape.

Note: It is not necessary to weight the foil and dough with beans.

6. Bake in the preheated oven, on the lowest shelf, for 15 minutes. Remove from the oven, lift out the foil and return the shell to the oven for 5 minutes. Remove and cool. While the crust cools, make the filling.

7. Preheat the oven to 350 F.

8. Sauté the onions in the butter for 20 minutes without allowing them to brown. Pour them into a strainer and drain off the butter.

Note: Save the onion-flavored butter for cooking.

9. Fry the bacon until crisp. Drain on paper towels.

10. Scatter the bacon, onion and cheese slices over the bottom of the cooled crust.

11. In a mixing bowl, combine the cornstarch, salt, pepper and a grind or two of nutmeg. Add enough cream to make a smooth paste, then add the rest of the cream along with the milk, eggs and egg yolk. Mix well, but do not beat.

12. Strain the egg-milk mixture into the pastry shell. With a spoon, skim any foam from the surface (foam toughens when baked).

13. Bake in the preheated oven for about 20 minutes, then reduce the heat to 325 F. and bake about 10 minutes longer, or until the custard is set. Cool. Serve warm.

Note: There will probably be some custard left over. You cannot possibly fill the shell to the top and then move it to the oven without spilling. Therefore, as the quiche cooks, gradually add the leftover custard to the middle of the pie, thus making the pie thicker and better.

SPINACH QUICHE

Marion Lear Swaybill

One 9" tart

1 PACKAGE (10 OUNCES) FROZEN, CHOPPED SPINACH
3 TABLESPOONS BUTTER
2 TABLESPOONS CHOPPED SCALLIONS
3 EGGS, LIGHTLY BEATEN
1½ CUPS HEAVY CREAM
½ TEASPOON SALT
½ TEASPOON PEPPER
½ TEASPOON GROUND NUTMEG
ONE 9" PARTIALLY BAKED TART SHELL (PREFERABLY HOMEMADE)
¼ CUP GRATED GRUYÈRE CHEESE

1. Preheat the oven to 375 F.

2. Thaw the spinach slightly and cut it into 12 pieces.

3. In a pan, heat 2 tablespoons of the butter until foamy. Add the scallions and cook briefly. Add the spinach and cook until all of the liquid evaporates.

4. In a bowl, combine the eggs, cream and seasonings. Add the spinach mixture and stir well.

5. Pour into the pie crust, top with the cheese and dot with the remaining table-spoon of butter.

6. Bake for 30 minutes, or until a knife inserted in the center comes out clean.

CLAM PIE

Ruth Spear

6 servings

Clam pie is particularly indigenous to Eastern Long Island and, like clam chowder, its variations have passionate exponents. Some use all "quahogs" or hard clams. Others use both hard and soft clams. Additional flourishes include adding diced, cooked bacon, grated green pepper or chopped celery. The pie can have one crust or two, and may be made richer by adding egg and cream. One old East Hampton recipe directs that the pie be served with hot chicken gravy. The old recipes are uniform in omitting salt, but you may add some if you wish.

2 CUPS SHUCKED CLAMS, DRAINED AND CUT UP (18 TO 24 CHERRY-STONES, OR 1 DOZEN QUAHOGS)
1 MEDIUM-SIZED ONION, CUT UP
1 MEDIUM-SIZED POTATO, PEELED AND CUT UP
1 EGG
¼ CUP CREAM
¾ TEASPOON POULTRY SEASONING
FRESHLY GROUND BLACK PEPPER, TO TASTE
2 TABLESPOONS CHOPPED PARSLEY
1 RECIPE RICH PIE PASTRY (PAGE 00)
2 TABLESPOONS BUTTER

1. Preheat the oven to 400 F.

2. Put the clams, onions and potato through a meat grinder, or chop coarsely in a food processor.

3. Beat the egg with the cream and add it to the clam mixture along with the seasonings and parsley. Let the mixture stand while you prepare the pie pastry.

4. Line a 9" pie pan with the pastry, fill with the clam mixture, dot with butter and cover with the pastry top. Crimp the edges to make a few slits to let the steam escape.

5. Bake in the preheated oven for 10 minutes, then lower the heat to 350 F. and bake an additional 30 to 35 minutes.

6. Serve the pie piping hot.

LITTLE PIZZAS (PIZZATINE)

Nicola Zanghi

6 to 12 pies

Pizza is made in the form of small, individual pies along the Mediterranean coasts of France and Italy. Here, in addition to the basic pizza dough recipe, I have suggested four different fillings that you might try. I haven't given any quantities for the filling ingredients, however, as this is really a matter of personal judgment and taste. *Pizzatine* make a great late night snack, and if made a little larger can be served for lunch or a light dinner.

Dough:
1 PACKAGE ACTIVE DRY YEAST
1 CUP WARM WATER
1 POUND (ABOUT 3½ CUPS) FLOUR, SIFTED
1 TEASPOON SALT
1 EGG, LIGHTLY BEATEN
3 TABLESPOONS OLIVE OIL

Tomato Sauce:
2 TABLESPOONS OLIVE OIL
2 TABLESPOONS MINCED SCALLION (WHITE PART ONLY)
1 SMALL CLOVE GARLIC, MINCED
2 TABLESPOONS MARSALA
2 CUPS PEELED, COARSELY CHOPPED AND DRAINED PLUM TOMATOES

$^1/_8$ TEASPOON OREGANO
¼ TEASPOON DRIED OR 1 TABLESPOON MINCED FRESH BASIL
¼ TEASPOON FENNEL SEEDS
SALT
FRESHLY GROUND BLACK PEPPER

Fillings:
CHEESE: DICED MOZZARELLA WITH A SPRINKLING OF PARMESAN
PUTANESCA: SLICED BLACK OLIVES, ANCHOVY FILLETS, CAPERS
SALUMERIA: DICED BOILED HAM, *PROSCIUTTO*, SAUSAGE, BACON
CAMPAGNOLO: CHOPPED GREEN PEPPER AND ONION, SLICED MUSHROOMS, OLIVE OIL

1. Dissolve the yeast in the warm water and set aside to proof.

2. Mix together the flour, salt, egg and oil. Stir in the yeast mixture and work the dough until it is elastic, about 10 minutes. Place in an oiled bowl, cover with a dry cloth and set in a warm place for 1 hour, or until doubled in bulk.

3. Meanwhile, prepare the tomato sauce. In a heavy-bottomed saucepan, heat the olive oil and sauté the scallion over medium heat until limp. Add the garlic and sauté for 2 minutes. Add the Marsala and let the mixture reduce for approximately 2 to 3 minutes.

4. Add the tomatoes, bring to a boil, then reduce the heat and simmer for 15 minutes.

5. Add the oregano, basil and fennel seeds. Taste for salt (you should need about ¼ teaspoon) and season with 3 or 4 twists of the peppermill. Simmer for 5 more minutes. Reserve.

6. Once the dough has risen, cut it into pieces the size of a peach; knead and shape into balls. Place on a tray, cover with a dry cloth and let rest 30 minutes.

   Note: The dough must be allowed to rise for the length of time specified, or your pizza may be chewy and tough.

7a. Meanwhile, prepare the fillings of your choice. Preparing the cheese and *putanesca* fillings is a simple matter of dicing, slicing and grating the various ingredients as listed.

7b. If using uncured or uncooked ham or sausages for the *salumeria* filling, they must be sautéed before topping the *pizzatine* with them. It is not necessary to fry the bacon, however, as it will get sufficiently cooked in the oven.

7c. To prepare the *campagnolo* filling, sauté the pepper, onion and mushrooms in a little olive oil until soft. Reserve.

8. Preheat the oven to 475 F.

9. Flour a work surface liberally. Stretch the balls of dough into 6'' to 8'' rounds and place them on a baking sheet.

10. Spread tomato sauce over each round and sprinkle them with the filling or fillings of your choice. Bake in the preheated oven for 15 minutes, until lightly browned and crisp around the edges.

CRAB QUICHE

Alma Lach

6 to 8 servings

1 ONION, THINLY SLICED
1 SHALLOT, MINCED
1 TABLESPOON BUTTER
DASH OF SALT
FRESHLY GROUND WHITE PEPPER,
  TO TASTE
2 TABLESPOONS SHERRY
1 TABLESPOON TOMATO PURÉE
¼ CUP GRATED PARMESAN

1 PARTIALLY BAKED 8'' TART SHELL
  (PAGE 00)
¼ POUND LUMP CRAB MEAT, WELL
  CLEANED
2 TEASPOONS CORNSTARCH
1 CUP HEAVY CREAM
1 CUP MILK
3 WHOLE EGGS
1 EGG YOLK

1. Preheat the oven to 350 F.

2. Sauté the onion and shallot in the butter until softened. Stir in the salt, pepper, sherry and tomato purée and boil to reduce the sherry. Cool.

3. Sprinkle the Parmesan over the bottom of the partially baked crust. Add the sautéed onion mixture and then the crab meat.

4. In a bowl, combine the cornstarch with enough cream to make a smooth paste. Add the remaining cream and milk, then the eggs and egg yolk, mixing well. Strain as much of the mixture into the pie shell as will fit without danger of spilling over on the trip from countertop to oven.

5. Set the pie in the oven and add any remaining custard if there is room.

   Note: If all the custard will not fit in the shell, gradually add it to the center of the pie as it cooks. This technique will give you a very full pie.

6. Bake in the preheated oven for about 20 minutes, then reduce the heat to 325 F. and bake about 10 minutes longer, or until the custard is set. Cool and serve warm.

Sweet Pies and Tarts

DEEP-DISH BLACKBERRY AND APPLE PIE

Maurice Moore-Betty

6 servings

Filling:
6 GREENING OR OTHER COOKING
  APPLES
1 PINT FRESH BLACKBERRIES
½ CUP SUGAR
8 WHOLE CLOVES
2 STICKS CINNAMON, BROKEN IN
  HALF
GRATED RIND OF 1 LEMON

Pastry:
2 CUPS ALL-PURPOSE FLOUR
½ TEASPOON SALT

3 TABLESPOONS CHILLED SHORT-
  ENING
8 TABLESPOONS (1 STICK)
  CHILLED BUTTER
3 TABLESPOONS ICE WATER,
  APPROXIMATELY

Glaze:
¼ CUP HEAVY CREAM
1 EGG YOLK
SUPERFINE SUGAR

1. Peel and core the apples and cut into thin slices.

2. In a bowl, toss the apples, blackberries, sugar, cloves, cinnamon sticks and grated lemon rind.

3. Sift the flour and salt into a mixing bowl. Add the shortening and chip the cold butter into the bowl. Cut in with a pastry blender until the mixture is coarse and mealy. Add enough ice water to form a ball, handling the pastry as little as possible.

   Note: Also use as little water as possible to bind the pastry.

4. Transfer the dough to a floured board. Spread it out once with the heel of the hand for a final blending of the flour and butter. Gather it into a ball and seal in a plastic bag or wrap. Refrigerate for at least 2 hours.

5. Preheat the oven to 350 F.

6. Fill a deep pie dish with the sliced apple and blackberry mixture, mounding it to form a dome. Add enough water to half fill the dish.

7. Roll out the chilled pastry to a thickness of about ¼". Moisten the edge of the dish. Lay the pastry over the apples and blackberries and press it to the rim of the dish.

8. From the pastry trimmings, cut a strip the same width as the dish rim. Moisten

the edge of the pastry lid and lay the strip neatly around the rim, pressing so that it makes a firm contact. Crimp the edge with your fingers.

9. Mix the cream with the egg yolk and brush the entire surface of the pastry with the mixture.

10. Roll out the remaining pastry scraps and make decorative cut-outs. Arrange them on top of the pie and brush with the egg-cream mixture.

   Note: A steam vent is not necessary.

11. Bake in the preheated oven for 1 hour. (If the pastry takes on too much color, cover it with a sheet of foil.)

12. Dust the pie with fine sugar while still hot. Serve with heavy clotted cream, *crème fraîche* or just heavy cream.

CURRANT TART

Florence Fabricant

8 servings

1 CUP DRIED CURRANTS
¼ CUP DARK RUM
PASTRY FOR A 9'', SINGLE-CRUST PIE
4 TABLESPOONS (½ STICK) BUTTER,
   SOFTENED
1 CUP DARK BROWN SUGAR
1 CUP LIGHT CORN SYRUP
3 EGGS, LIGHTLY BEATEN
1 TEASPOON VANILLA EXTRACT

1. Combine the currants and rum and set aside.

2. Preheat the oven to 450 F.

3. Roll out the pastry and fit it into a 9'' or 10'' flan ring or tart pan. Prick it all over and line it with foil weighted with dry beans or with aluminum pastry weights.

4. Bake for 5 minutes, remove the foil and beans, reprick the pastry and bake another 2 to 3 minutes, until the pastry is done. Remove from the oven and lower the temperature to 375 F.

5. Cream the butter and sugar together. Stir in the syrup and eggs. Add the vanilla and the currants and rum.

6. Pour the mixture into the prepared pastry shell. Bake for 30 minutes, until the top is brown and the filling fairly firm.

7. Cool to room temperature before serving. Whipped cream is a fine accompaniment.

Note: The tart may be frozen after it is completely baked.

RASPBERRY BARQUETTES

Susan Lipke

12 barquettes

Pastry Crust:
8 OUNCES (APPROXIMATELY 1¾
  CUPS) UNBLEACHED, ALL-PURPOSE
  FLOUR
2 TABLESPOONS SUGAR
PINCH OF SALT
8 TABLESPOONS (1 STICK) UN-
  SALTED BUTTER, WELL CHILLED
2½ TABLESPOONS VEGETABLE
  SHORTENING, WELL CHILLED
1 EGG YOLK
⅓ CUP ICE WATER

Almond Cream:
1 EGG YOLK
3 TABLESPOONS SUGAR
2 TABLESPOONS UNSALTED BUTTER
1 OUNCE (¼ CUP) PULVERIZED AL-
  MONDS

Other Ingredients:
½ CUP RASPBERRY JELLY
1 CUP RASPBERRIES, WASHED AND
  WELL DRAINED

1. Toss the flour, sugar and salt together in a bowl. Cut the butter and shortening into small pieces and add them to the bowl. Using your fingertips, a
   pastry blender or two knives, rapidly work or cut the fat into the flour until
   the bits of butter are the size of peas.

2. Beat the egg yolk with the ice water and add it to the flour mixture. Stir together quickly with a fork until all of the liquid has been incorporated and all
   of the flour moistened. If the mixture appears too dry, dribble in a little more
   ice water.

3. Gather the dough into a ball, place it on a pastry board and quickly rub egg-
   sized lumps away from you with the heel of the hand. Gather the pastry back
   into a ball, sprinkle with flour, cover with plastic wrap and refrigerate for at
   least 2 hours.

4. To make the almond cream, beat the egg yolk and half of the sugar together
   with a wire whisk until thick and pale yellow in color.

5. Cream the butter with the remaining sugar, then blend it into the yolk mixture
   with a rubber spatula. Stir in the almonds and refrigerate the mixture until
   ready to use.

6. Butter the insides of twelve 4" to 4½"-long *barquette* tins (shallow, oval "boats")
   and the outsides of twelve more.

   Note: The extra tins are used to weight the pastry during its first baking. If
   you have only twelve *barquette* tins, make the pastry boats in two batches of
   six each.

7. Divide the pastry in half and wrap and freeze one half for future use. Roll
   the other half of the pastry into a sheet ⅛" thick. Using an oval pastry cutter
   —or the tip of a sharp knife and an inverted *barquette* tin as a guide—cut the
   pastry into 12 ovals approximately ¼" bigger around than the *barquettes*.

8. Press the pastry gently into the tins that are buttered on the inside. Trim the
   edges, if necessary (having used the right sized pastry cutter will eliminate
   this step), and prick each *barquette* with a fork. Press one of the empty tins
   into each pastry-lined *barquette*.

9. Place the *barquette* tins on a baking sheet and refrigerate for 30 to 60 minutes.

10. Preheat the oven to 375 F.

11. Bake the weighted *barquettes* for 5 minutes.

12. Remove the tin liners, prick the pastry again with a fork and return it to the oven for 1 minute longer, or until it just begins to set.

13. Remove the pastry from the oven and allow it to cool to lukewarm. Then, spread a teaspoon of the almond cream over the bottom of each *barquette* (making sure to leave room for the raspberries).

14. Return the *barquettes* to the oven and bake until the pastry is completely cooked and the almond cream has puffed and is golden brown, about 10 to 12 minutes.

    Note: Don't be alarmed if the almond cream puffs to the top of the *barquette*. Just use a little less the next time.

15. Take the *barquettes* from the oven, allow them to cool completely and remove them from the tins.

16. Meanwhile, make the glaze. Place the raspberry jelly in a small saucepan and boil it for several minutes, until thick. It should register about 230 F. on a candy thermometer.

17. Brush the hot glaze over the almond cream in each *barquette* and place as many raspberries as will fit comfortably on top of it. Dribble more glaze over the raspberries, and chill thoroughly before serving.

Note: The pastry recipe given is double the quantity necessary for 12 *barquettes* both because this specific combination of ingredients seems to make the best pastry, and because it is just as easy to make enough pastry for two recipes as for one. The extra pastry can be frozen, ready for your next tart. There will be enough to make a 9'' tart shell. Or, if you cut 1 or 2 ovals from the edges or scraps of dough of every sweet tart you make, and save them up in the freezer, you can eliminate making the pastry altogether the next time.

GREEN TOMATO PIE

Emanuel and Madeline Greenberg

6 to 8 servings

2 POUNDS GREEN TOMATOES*
¾ CUP PACKED BROWN SUGAR
½ CUP GRANULATED SUGAR
1 TEASPOON CINNAMON
½ TEASPOON GROUND GINGER
½ TEASPOON GROUND NUTMEG
½ TEASPOON SALT

1 TEASPOON GRATED ORANGE PEEL
1 TABLESPOON ORANGE JUICE
1 TABLESPOON LEMON JUICE
2 TABLESPOONS CORNSTARCH
PASTRY FOR A 9'', DOUBLE-CRUST PIE
1 TABLESPOON BUTTER

1. Place the tomatoes in a colander and immerse them in a large pot of rapidly boiling water for about 1 minute. Lift out the colander and immediately rinse the tomatoes with cold water. Peel off the skins, quarter them and scoop out the

Continued from preceding page

seeds. Thinly slice the tomatoes.

2. In a large bowl, combine the remaining ingredients, except the pastry and butter. Add the tomatoes, stir gently and let stand about 15 minutes.

3. Preheat the oven to 450 F.

4. Line a 9" pie pan with the rolled-out pastry. Spoon in the sliced tomato mixture; dot with butter. Cover with the top crust; trim and seal the edges. Cut several slashes in the top crust.

5. Place the pan in the preheated oven and bake 15 minutes. Reduce the heat to 350 F. and bake 35 to 40 minutes longer, until the crust is browned and the tomatoes are tender.

6. Serve warm or at room temperature. Accompany with a good cheddar cheese, if desired.

Note: For a chutney-like flavor, add 2 tablespoons of finely diced, candied ginger to the tomato mixture.

* Use tomatoes that are fully grown, but that have not yet started to turn color.

RICOTTA PIE

Eliza and Joshua Baer

One 9" pie

Crust:
8 TABLESPOONS (1 STICK) BUTTER
1½ CUPS UNBLEACHED WHITE FLOUR
¼ CUP BROWN SUGAR
6 TABLESPOONS ICE WATER, APPROXIMATELY
4 TABLESPOONS MARSALA (DRY OR SWEET)
2 EGG YOLKS
½ TEASPOON SALT
DASH OF FRESHLY GRATED NUTMEG

Filling:
5 CUPS FRESH RICOTTA CHEESE
¾ CUP HONEY (ONE OF THE LIGHTER VARIETIES SUCH AS CLOVER OR ORANGE BLOSSOM)

1 TABLESPOON UNBLEACHED WHITE FLOUR
½ TEASPOON SALT
2 TEASPOONS VANILLA EXTRACT
1 TEASPOON FRESHLY GRATED ORANGE RIND (USE A VERY FINE GRATING SURFACE)
1 TEASPOON FRESHLY GRATED LEMON RIND
4 EGG YOLKS
JUICE OF 1 LEMON
½ CUP GOLDEN RAISINS*
½ CUP SLIVERED, LIGHTLY TOASTED ALMONDS

1. Cut the butter into the flour and brown sugar.

2. When the butter lumps are pea-sized, make a well in the center of the mixture and fill it with the ice water, Marsala, egg yolks, salt and nutmeg.

3. With a large fork, toss the wet ingredients with the dry ingredients. As the

mass gets sticky, press it together with your hands. If the dough is too flaky, add more ice water.

4. Form the dough into a ball, put the ball in a plastic bag and chill it for at least 2 hours.

   Note: Overnight is even better. The longer the dough chills, the easier it will be to roll out.

5. Preheat the oven to 350 F.

6. Combine all of the filling ingredients except the raisins and almonds. Mix very well and taste; add more honey for a sweeter filling.

7. Stir in the almonds and raisins.

8. Roll out the chilled pie dough to a thickness of ¼'' to ½''. Lay the dough in a buttered 9'' pie pan. Trim the edges and crimp them.

9. Put the filling in the pie shell and spread it evenly. If there are any extra almond slivers, sprinkle them on top of the filling.

10. Bake the pie in the center of the preheated oven for about 1¼ hours. The pie is done when the cheese filling is slightly puffed and the crust is golden.

Note: This pie is most flavorful 10 to 15 minutes after baking. It is, however, excellent cold. Do not strive for a perfect, totally crisp crust the first few times you make it. The filling is so unusual, and so good, that it will "carry" the pie until you work out the perfect proportions for the crust, relative to your own oven, kitchen temperature and the speed at which you work.

* For special results, soak the raisins for 1 hour in ¼ cup Marsala.

RHUBARB-STRAWBERRY TART

Ruth Spear

8 servings

Rich Pie Pastry:
1½ CUPS UNBLEACHED FLOUR
2 EGG YOLKS
2 TABLESPOONS CONFECTIONERS' SUGAR
⅛ TEASPOON SALT
8 TABLESPOONS (1 STICK) BUTTER, CHILLED
3 TABLESPOONS WATER, APPROXIMATELY

Filling:
2 CUPS FRESH, YOUNG RHUBARB, CUT INTO ½'' CUBES
2 CUPS FRESH STRAWBERRIES, HALVED IF SMALL, QUARTERED IF LARGE
1 CUP SUGAR
¾ TEASPOON GROUND CARDAMOM
3 TABLESPOONS FLOUR
2 EGGS, LIGHTLY BEATEN

1. In a mixing bowl or the container of a food processor, combine the flour, yolks, sugar and salt.

2. Cut the butter into small pieces and add to the bowl. Work with the hands and add just enough water to make the pastry hold together, or process similarly by machine.

Continued from preceding page

3. Remove the dough, form it into a ball, sprinkle lightly with flour and wrap in waxed paper. Refrigerate for 2 to 3 hours.

4. Roll the dough out on a floured board and line a buttered, 10'' tart tin (with a removable bottom).

5. Preheat the oven to 400 F.

6. Put the rhubarb and strawberries in a mixing bowl.

7. In a small bowl, blend the sugar, cardamom and flour together, then toss with the fruit.

8. Add the eggs and blend thoroughly.

9. Pour this mixture into the prepared tart shell, smooth with a spatula and place on a baking sheet in the lower third of the oven. Bake for 40 minutes, or until the tart has set.

10. Remove from the oven, let cool for 5 minutes, then remove the sides of the tart tin. Serve slightly warm or at room temperature.

SPICY PUMPKIN NUT PIE

Jane Moulton

6 to 8 servings

2 EGGS
¾ CUP SUGAR
½ TEASPOON SALT
1 TABLESPOON CINNAMON
1½ TEASPOONS GROUND GINGER
½ TEASPOON GROUND CLOVES
½ TEASPOON GROUND NUTMEG
1 TEASPOON VANILLA
1 CAN (16 OUNCES) PUMPKIN

1 CAN (13 OUNCES) EVAPORATED (NOT SWEETENED CONDENSED) MILK
1 DEEP, 9'' PIE SHELL, UNBAKED
¼ CUP CHOPPED, CRYSTALLIZED GINGER
½ CUP CHOPPED WALNUTS OR PECANS

1. Preheat the oven to 425 F.

2. In a large mixer bowl, beat the eggs slightly, then mix in the sugar, salt, cinnamon, ginger, cloves, nutmeg and vanilla. Mix well.

3. Thoroughly blend in the pumpkin and stir in the milk.

4. Pour the filling into the unbaked pie shell.

5. Sprinkle the chopped ginger evenly over the surface. (It tends to collect in bunches if poured in with the filling.) Sprinkle on the nuts.

6. Bake in the preheated oven until the crust just begins to turn brown, about 13 minutes. Reduce the heat to 350 F. and bake about 45 minutes longer, until a knife inserted in the middle comes out clean.

7. Cool slightly on a rack and serve warm. Top with vanilla, butter pecan or toffee

ice cream, or whipped cream garnished with a sliver of crystallized ginger, if desired.

Note: To make ahead of time, freeze the pie shell without the filling. The filling may be made the day before and refrigerated. Stir before pouring it into the crust.

CHOCOLATE MOUSSE PIE

Florence Fabricant

One 9" pie

2 OUNCES SWEET CHOCOLATE
3 TABLESPOONS RUM OR COGNAC
ONE 9" PIE CRUST, FULLY BAKED
  AND COOLED
½ TABLESPOON (½ ENVELOPE) UN-
  FLAVORED GELATIN

4 OUNCES SEMISWEET CHOCOLATE
¼ CUP STRONG COFFEE
4 EGGS, SEPARATED
¼ CUP SUGAR
½ CUP HEAVY CREAM

1. Melt the sweet chocolate over hot water or very low heat. Stir in 1 tablespoon of the rum (or cognac). Spread this mixture over the bottom of the pie shell and set aside.

2. Soften the gelatin in the remaining 2 tablespoons of rum (or cognac) and set aside.

3. Melt the semisweet chocolate with the coffee over hot water or very low heat, stirring until smooth. Stir in the softened gelatin and continue stirring over very low heat until the gelatin dissolves.

   Note: It is essential to melt the chocolates and add the gelatin over extremely low heat. I use an electric coffee warmer. If too much heat is applied, the chocolate will become grainy, the gelatin rubbery and the two will not combine smoothly.

4. Beat in the egg yolks, one at a time, stirring until the mixture is smooth. Remove from the heat, transfer to a large bowl and set aside to cool to room temperature.

5. Whip the egg whites until they form soft peaks. Sprinkle on the sugar and beat until stiff but not dry.

6. Gently, but thoroughly, fold the egg whites into the cooled chocolate mixture. Spoon the mousse into the prepared pie shell and chill at least 4 hours.

7. The finished pie may be decorated with whipped cream. Whip the cream while the pie is chilling and place it in a strainer lined with cheesecloth and suspended over a bowl. Refrigerate at least 1 hour.

   Note: Suspending the whipped cream over a bowl drains off the whey, preventing the cream from becoming runny after the decorations are applied.

8. When the pie is fully chilled, pipe a border of whipped cream rosettes or flutings onto the pie.

DRIED APRICOT TARTLETS

Elizabeth Schneider Colchie

12 tartlets

8 TABLESPOONS (1 STICK) UN-
SALTED BUTTER, SOFTENED
⅔ CUP SUGAR
2 LARGE EGGS
½ TEASPOON ALMOND EXTRACT
¼ TEASPOON VANILLA EXTRACT
½ TEASPOON GRATED LEMON RIND
2 CUPS FLOUR
½ TEASPOON DOUBLE-ACTING
BAKING POWDER
¼ TEASPOON SALT

2 CUPS (ABOUT 11 OUNCES) DRIED
APRICOT HALVES ("TENDERIZED"
OR MOISTPACK), COARSELY CHOPPED
1 CUP WATER
⅓ CUP HONEY
1 TABLESPOON LEMON JUICE
2 TABLESPOONS BRANDY
MILK
⅓ CUP CHOPPED OR SLIVERED AL-
MONDS (BLANCHED OR NOT)
CONFECTIONERS' SUGAR

1. In the bowl of an electric mixer, cream the butter until light. Gradually beat in the sugar, beating until light and fluffy.

2. Beat in the eggs, one at a time. Then add the almond and vanilla extracts and lemon rind.

3. Sift together the flour, baking powder and salt. Gradually add the flour to the creamed butter mixture with the machine running at the lowest speed.

4. Form the dough into a rough rectangle and wrap it in floured plastic wrap or in waxed paper. Chill for at least 2 hours.

5. In a heavy saucepan, combine the apricots, water, honey, and lemon juice. Bring to a boil, stirring, then cover and simmer for 15 minutes, or until the fruit is tender. Add the brandy and let the mixture cool.

6. Preheat the oven to 350 F.

7. Butter twelve fluted tartlet molds, each about 3½" in diameter and with a capacity of approximately ¼ cup.

8. Cut the dough into four parts; refrigerate one quarter. Cut each of the three remaining quarters into four parts. Roll each part into a ball, then press it out on a floured surface to form a circle roughly the diameter of the molds. Fit a dough circle evenly into a mold, pressing the pastry lightly into each curve. Repeat the process to line all of the molds.

9. Divide the cooled apricot filling among the molds (about 1 heaping tablespoon each) and spread it evenly over the pastry shell.

10. On a lightly floured surface, roll out the remaining, chilled dough to form a rectangle approximately 13" to 14" long and 3½" wide. Cut the dough crosswise into 24 strips, using a fluted pastry wheel, if available.

11. Place two strips of the dough over each tartlet forming a cross. Press the ends very lightly onto the rim. Brush the strips with milk, and sprinkle with almonds. Place the tartlets on a baking sheet.

12. Bake in the preheated oven until golden, about 30 to 35 minutes. Let the tartlets rest for 5 minutes on a rack before slipping them out of the molds. Sprinkle the tops lightly with confectioners' sugar before serving.

FRESH PEACH PIE

Paul Rubinstein

6 servings

1½ CUPS ALL-PURPOSE FLOUR
1 CUP GRANULATED SUGAR
4 TABLESPOONS (½ STICK) VEGETA-
   BLE SHORTENING, CHILLED
4 TABLESPOONS (½ STICK) UNSALTED
   BUTTER, CHILLED
2 TABLESPOONS ICE WATER

4 EGG YOLKS
1½ CUPS MILK
1 TABLESPOON VANILLA EXTRACT
4 WHOLE, JUST-RIPE PEACHES
½ CUP PEACH JAM OR PEACH
   PRESERVES

1. Into a mixing bowl, sift 1 cup of the flour with 2 tablespoons of the sugar.

2. Cut in the shortening and 3 tablespoons of the chilled butter with a pastry blender. Then add the ice water and gather the dough into a rough ball. Knead it on a lightly floured pastry board to achieve a smooth, well blended dough.

3. Wrap the dough in waxed paper and refrigerate for 30 minutes.

4. Preheat the oven to 400 F.

5. Roll the dough out into a 10'' to 10½'' circle and line a 9'' pie dish with it, crimping the edges along the lip of the dish. (The dough is very short and may have to be patched. Simply press an extra scrap of dough over any tears.)

6. Perforate the bottom of the dough with a fork at 1'' intervals. Line the dough with a sheet of buttered aluminum foil (buttered side down) and weight the foil with dried beans or marbles.

7. Bake the pie shell in the preheated oven for 8 minutes, or until it is set.

8. Take the pie dish out of the oven, carefully remove the foil and weights, prick the bottom of the pastry again, and return it to the oven for about 10 to 12 minutes, until the crust is golden brown. Remove the dish from the oven and let the pie shell stand until it has cooled to room temperature.

9. With an electric mixer, beat the egg yolks, adding ¾ cup of the remaining sugar a little at a time until the mixture is smooth and forms a ribbon when allowed to run from a spoon.

10. Beat in the remaining ½ cup of flour.

11. Bring the milk to a boil and pour it into the egg yolk mixture in a thin stream, running the mixer the whole time. At first the thick mixture will strain the machine, but the pastry cream will thin out as you pour in the milk.

12. Pour the pastry cream into a heavy saucepan and bring it to a boil, stirring vigorously with a wire whisk until it thickens to a heavy consistency and beating becomes difficult.

13. Off the heat, beat in the remaining tablespoon of butter and the vanilla extract. Let the cream cool to lukewarm.

14. Peel the peaches, cut them in half and remove the pits. Then cut the peaches into ¼''-thick crescent-shaped slices.

15. Fill the baked pie crust with the vanilla-flavored pastry cream to within ¼'' of the top. Arrange the peach slices on top of the cream in an overlapping pattern.

16. Rub the peach jam through a sieve into a small, heavy enameled or stainless-steel saucepan. Add the remaining 2 tablespoons of sugar and bring this glaze mixture to a boil. Boil for 1 minute and remove from the heat. Let the glaze cool for 2 to 3 minutes.

17. Carefully pour the peach glaze over the peach slices to form a thin coating over the entire surface of the pie. If you seem to run short, quickly spread out the glaze, before it cools, with a pastry brush.

18. The pie is now ready to serve and may stand at room temperature for several hours or even overnight. It should *not* be refrigerated.

PECAN PIE

Marion Lear Swaybill

One 10" pie

Crust:
1 CUP FLOUR, SIFTED TWICE
½ TEASPOON SALT
⅓ CUP VEGETABLE SHORTENING
3 TABLESPOONS ICE WATER

Filling:
6 EGGS
¾ CUP PACKED DARK BROWN SUGAR
¾ CUP WHITE SUGAR
1½ CUPS DARK CORN SYRUP
1½ TABLESPOONS FLOUR
¾ TEASPOON SALT
4½ TABLESPOONS BUTTER, MELTED
3 TEASPOONS VANILLA EXTRACT
1½ CUPS (6 OUNCES) PECANS, CUT INTO PIECES

1. Sift together the flour and salt. With a pastry blender, cut in the vegetable shortening until the mixture is pebble-like in texture. Sprinkle on the water and toss with forks until a ball forms. Do not handle.

2. Flatten the pastry ball into a fat disc between two pieces of waxed paper and refrigerate at least 1 hour.

3. Preheat the oven to 350 F.

4. On a well floured board, roll out the dough to a thickness of $1/_8$". Press into a 10" metal (or Pyrex) pie pan and flute the edges.

5. To make the filling, beat the eggs, add all of the filling ingredients except the pecans and mix until well blended. Add the pecans and mix again.

6. Pour the filling into the prepared shell (the pecans will rise to the top) and bake in the preheated oven for 40 minutes. To test for doneness, press the back of a spoon in the center of the filling. If it feels solid, the pie is done.

7. Serve with sweetened whipped cream or vanilla ice cream. To reheat, place the pie in a 300 F. oven for 10 minutes.

Note: I have had great success doubling this recipe and making it in an 11" x 1½"-deep tart pan. Doubled, it will serve 12 to 16 people. It also travels well.

HOT APPLE TARTS WITH CRÈME FRÂICHE

Susan Lipke

4 tarts

Crème Frâiche:
1 PINT HEAVY CREAM, PREFERABLY
  NOT ULTRA-PASTEURIZED
1 TABLESPOON BUTTERMILK OR
  PLAIN YOGURT

Puff Pastry:
1⅓ CUPS (6¾ OUNCES) PLUS ½ CUP
  UNBLEACHED ALL-PURPOSE FLOUR
⅓ CUP (1¼ OUNCES) SIFTED CAKE
  FLOUR
¾ TEASPOON SALT

½ POUND PLUS 2½ TABLESPOONS
  UNSALTED BUTTER
½ CUP ICE WATER, APPROXIMATELY

Filling:
1 EGG, LIGHTLY BEATEN
1 LARGE FIRM APPLE, SUCH AS
  GOLDEN DELICIOUS, PEELED AND
  THINLY SLICED
8 TEASPOONS UNSALTED BUTTER,
  MELTED
8 TEASPOONS GRANULATED SUGAR

1. Make the *crème frâiche* the day (or several days) before you plan to serve the apple tarts. Place the heavy cream in a glass jar, add the buttermilk (or yogurt), cover and shake well. Leave at room temperature until the cream thickens, at least 6 hours (in warm weather) or up to 24 hours. Shake again and refrigerate. The cream will become much thicker as it chills.

2. In a bowl, toss together the 1⅓ cups all-purpose flour, the cake flour and salt. Cut 2½ tablespoons of the butter into small pieces, add them to the bowl and rapidly cut into the flour, until the mixture resembles coarse cornmeal. Make a well in the center, add the water and stir with a fork until all the water is incorporated. If the dough seems too dry, sprinkle on a little more water.

3. Gather the dough into a ball, place on a lightly floured surface and knead a few times to blend the ingredients together well. Wrap in waxed paper and refrigerate while preparing the butter.

4. Place the remaining ½ pound of butter on a work surface and beat with a rolling pin until it begins to get malleable. Sprinkle on the remaining ¼ cup of flour and knead it into the butter, working with the heels of your hands. When all the flour has been incorporated and the butter is quite malleable but still cold, form it into a patty and place at the edge of the work surface.

5. Remove the dough from the refrigerator and roll it into a rough circle or rectangle on a lightly floured surface. Place the butter in the center of the dough and fold the edges of the pastry over it, overlapping them slightly. Pinch the edges of the dough together well to enclose the butter completely.

6. Beat the pastry package lightly with a rolling pin to get it started. Then carefully roll it into a rectangle approximately 6" x 18", dusting lightly with flour, if necessary.

7. Carefully brush any flour from the surface of the pastry. Starting from a narrow end, fold the upper third of the rectangle over the center third and sweep all the flour from the exposed undersurface. Then fold the lower third of the pastry over the middle, making three equal layers. Give the pastry a quarter turn, so that one of the open ends faces you and gently press down on each open end with a rolling pin, to seal it. Repeat the rolling and folding process one

Continued from preceding page

more time, always being sure to brush the flour from the dough before folding.

Note: It is very important to brush the flour from the surface of the dough before folding. If it gets trapped between the layers, the puff pastry will be tough.

8. Wrap the pastry in waxed paper and refrigerate for 1 hour.

9. Roll and fold the pastry two more times, exactly as in Step 6, for a total of four turns. Refrigerate for at least 1 hour before proceeding.

10. Brush a large baking sheet with cold water.

11. Roll the pastry into a large rectangle 1/8" thick. Brush any flour from the surface and, using a very sharp knife and a lid or plate for a guide, cut four 5½" to 6" rounds from the sheet of pastry. Transfer them to the moistened baking sheet, being careful not to touch the cut edges of the pastry en route.

12. With your fingertips, gently push the centers of the pastry rounds outward, making them approximately ½" larger in diameter. Do not touch the pastry within 1" of the edge, as this will form the rim of the tart. Prick the depressed centers of the circles (not the rims), cover with a sheet of waxed paper and refrigerate for at least 1 hour.

13. Preheat the oven to 450 F.

14. When ready to prepare the tarts, remove the sheet of pastry rounds from the refrigerator and brush the rims with the beaten egg, being careful not to let it run down the cut edges of the pastry.

15. Arrange a layer of apple slices on each round, overlapping them. They should come to within no more than ¾" of the edges. Spoon 2 teaspoons of melted butter over the apples on each tart, and sprinkle 2 teaspoons of sugar over that. Do not dribble any butter or sugar on the rims.

16. Bake for 6 to 7 minutes in the preheated oven, then reduce the heat to 400 F. and bake 10 to 12 minutes longer, until puffed and golden brown.

17. Serve *immediately* with a generous scoop of *crème fraîche* over each portion.

ORANGE TART

Nan Mabon

6 servings

1 RECIPE PUFF PASTRY (PAGE 37)
1 EGG YOLK, BEATEN WITH 1 TEA-
 SPOON WATER
1 CUP MILK
1 TABLESPOON GRATED ORANGE RIND
3 EGG YOLKS

¼ CUP SUGAR
2 TABLESPOONS CORNSTARCH
2 TABLESPOONS ORANGE LIQUEUR
1 JAR (11 OUNCES) ORANGE SLICES
 IN SUGAR SYRUP*
½ CUP APRICOT JAM

1. Roll out the puff pastry into a rectangle $1/8$'' thick and measuring approximately 12½'' x 8½''. Using a very sharp knife, cut a 9'' x 5'' rectangle of dough from the center of the sheet of pastry. Then cut two ¾''-wide, 9''-long strips and two ¾''-wide, 5''-long strips from the remaining dough to build the sides of the pastry shell.

2. Place the large rectangle of dough on a baking sheet. Brush a ¾''-wide strip along the border of the pastry with the egg yolk wash, being careful not to let it drip down the cut edge of the pastry.

   Note: If the egg drips down the sides, it will seal together the many layers of pastry and prevent the dough from puffing properly as it bakes.

3. Place the dough strips flat along the corresponding edges of the rectangle, overlapping the ends at each corner, and press them very firmly into place with the back of a fork.

4. Prick the bottom of the pastry shell with a form, spread it with foil—being careful not to dislodge the sides—and weight down the foil with dried beans or rice. Refrigerate for 1 hour.

5. In a heavy-bottomed saucepan, beat the milk with the grated orange rind.

6. In another saucepan, beat the egg yolks with the sugar until blended, then whisk in the cornstarch.

7. Pour in a little of the hot milk (about ⅓ cup) through a strainer into the egg yolk mixture, then slowly add the rest. Be sure to strain out all the particles of orange rind.

8. Return the egg yolk mixture to a burner and stir constantly over moderate heat until it forms a very thick pastry cream.

9. Immediately scrape the pastry cream into a small container or mixing bowl and let it cool.

10. Stir in the orange liqueur and refrigerate.

11. Preheat the oven to 425 F.

12. Place the puff pastry (with the foil and weights) in the center of the oven and bake for 20 minutes. Remove the foil and weights, prick again with a fork and lower the heat to 400 F. Bake 25 minutes longer, or until nicely browned. Cool.

13. Drain the orange slices and, if necessary, slice them even thinner; they should be about $1/8$'' thick.

14. Heat the apricot jam until it melts, then strain. Brush the jam over the bottom and sides of the puff pastry shell.

15. About an hour before serving, spread the chilled pastry cream over the bottom of the shell and arrange slightly overlapping slices of orange in long rows on top, so that the pastry cream is covered.

Note: Although the tart was designed for a puff pastry shell, it can also be made with any pie crust prebaked in a flan form.

* If you can't locate orange slices preserved in syrup, try cutting 2 fresh unpeeled oranges crosswise into thin slices and poach them in a homemade syrup until the rind is tender and edible.

LATTICED BLUEBERRY PIE WITH ALMOND CRUST

Elizabeth Schneider Colchie

One 9" pie

Pastry:
1 CUP ALL-PURPOSE FLOUR
¾ CUP CAKE FLOUR
2 TABLESPOONS PLUS 2 TEASPOONS SUGAR
¼ TEASPOON SALT
6 TABLESPOONS (¾ STICK) BUTTER, CHILLED AND CUT INTO SMALL PIECES
4 TABLESPOONS VEGETABLE SHORTENING, CHILLED AND CUT INTO SMALL PIECES
½ CUP FINELY GROUND, UNBLANCHED ALMONDS

1 LARGE EGG
2 TABLESPOONS CREAM
½ TEASPOON ALMOND EXTRACT
½ TEASPOON VANILLA EXTRACT
1 EGG WHITE

Filling:
3 TABLESPOONS LEMON JUICE
2½ TABLESPOONS CORNSTARCH
⅔ CUP SUGAR
3½ CUPS BLUEBERRIES, CLEANED

1. Into a bowl, sift the flour, cake flour, 2 tablespoons of the sugar and the salt.

2. With a pastry blender, cut in the butter and shortening to make even particles the size of oatmeal flakes. Stir in the almonds.

3. In a small bowl, beat together the egg, cream and almond and vanilla extracts. Add gradually, a tablespoon at a time, to the flour mixture, tossing with a fork to mix well.

4. Gather the dough into a ball, wrap in plastic and chill 1 hour or more.

5. Preheat the oven to 400 F.

6. Cut off about two-thirds of the pastry and refrigerate the remainder. Roll out the dough to form a circle about 11" in diameter. Fit it into a buttered, 9" tart pan with a removable bottom. With a fork, prick the dough at ½" intervals, line the shell with foil, and fill with beans to weight down the crust. Bake in the middle level of the preheated oven for 8 minutes. Then, remove the beans and foil.

7. Beat the egg white with 2 teaspoons of sugar. Paint the bottom of the crust with some of this glaze and reserve the remainder.

8. Return to the oven and bake for 2 minutes longer. Remove and cool. (Do not turn off the oven.)

9. In a bowl, combine the lemon juice, cornstarch and sugar; stir to blend. Add the berries and mix well. Let stand for 30 minutes.

10. Raise the oven temperature to 425 F.

11. Roll out the remaining pastry on a sheet of floured waxed paper to form a circle about 10" in diameter. Cut it into 12 strips of equal width with a fluted pastry cutter.

12. Pour the berries into the cooled shell. Moisten both ends of a long strip of pastry with water and center it over the berries, pressing the ends down well. Continue with the remaining strips, forming a lattice pattern over the berries.

13. Beat the remaining egg white glaze to a froth and brush it gently over the lattice.

14. Bake the pie on the lower rack of the oven for 15 minutes. Lower the heat to 375 F. and bake the pie for 30 minutes more, until browned and bubbling. If the edges of the pie become too brown, protect them with strips of foil.

15. Cool on a rack and unmold carefully.

LEMON TART

Susan Lipke

One 9" tart

1 CUP WATER
1½ CUPS SUGAR
3 LARGE, FIRM LEMONS*

Pastry Cream:
3 EGG YOLKS
¼ CUP SUGAR
¼ TEASPOON VANILLA EXTRACT
1½ TABLESPOONS CORNSTARCH

1 CUP BOILING MILK
1½ TABLESPOONS STRAINED FRESH
  LEMON JUICE

2 TABLESPOONS STRAINED APRICOT
  PRESERVES
ONE 9" FULLY-COOKED, SWEET TART
  SHELL**

1. In a small saucepan, combine the water with the sugar, bring to a boil and simmer for 5 to 10 minutes.

2. Meanwhile, cut the lemons into $^3/_{16}$"-thick slices and carefully remove all of the seeds.

3. Add the lemon slices to the sugar syrup, pushing them down with a wooden spoon so that all of the slices are submerged. Simmer gently for about 5 minutes, then remove the pan from the heat and allow the lemon slices to cool in the syrup.

4. Arrange the cooled slices on a wire rack over a baking pan to drain. Cover with a sheet of waxed paper and refrigerate. Reserve the syrup.

5. Meanwhile, make the pastry cream. In a small bowl, beat together the egg yolks, sugar and vanilla with a wire whisk, until the mixture forms a ribbon. Sift in the cornstarch and blend it into the other ingredients with a whisk.

6. Scrape the mixture into a small, heavy-bottomed stainless, enameled or tinned saucepan and add the boiling milk all at once, whisking. Place over medium heat and cook, whisking constantly, until the mixture thickens, curdles and then smooths out again. Switch from a whisk to a wooden spoon and, stirring constantly, boil for 2 to 3 minutes longer. Remove from the heat and blend in the lemon juice.

7. Place a sheet of plastic wrap right on the surface of the custard to keep a skin from forming and refrigerate it until thoroughly chilled.

8. When ready to assemble the tart, place ½ cup of the reserved syrup in a small

Continued from preceding page

saucepan along with the apricot preserves and boil to a glaze consistency (about 230 F. on a candy thermometer). Keep warm.

9. Beat up the chilled pastry cream to loosen it, then spread it in the bottom of the tart shell. Arrange the drained lemon slices in overlapping circles over the pastry cream and brush with the warm glaze. Refrigerate until ready to serve.

* The lemons must be very fresh and firm. If they are not, they tend to disintegrate when cooked in the sugar syrup.

** Make the pastry as for the Raspberry Barquettes, page 28, and divide it in half. Chill and roll it as directed, then line a 9'' tart mold or flan form with the pastry, crimp the edges, prick the bottom and return it to the refrigerator to rest for another 30 to 60 minutes. Weight the shell with waxed paper or foil and beans and bake at 450 F. for 10 minutes. Remove the foil and beans, prick the bottom of the shell again and bake, empty, about 10 minutes longer, until golden brown and crisp.

CHERRY COBBLER

Carol Cutler

10 to 12 servings

8 TABLESPOONS (1 STICK) BUTTER
1 CUP FLOUR
1 CUP SUGAR
3 TEASPOONS BAKING POWDER
¼ TEASPOON SALT
1 CUP MILK
½ TEASPOON VANILLA EXTRACT
2 POUNDS FRESH CHERRIES
1 PINT HEAVY CREAM, WHIPPED AND
    SWEETENED (OPTIONAL)

1. Preheat the oven to 375 F.

2. In a 9'' x 13'' pan, melt the butter; tilt the pan so that the butter completely covers the bottom.

3. Into a bowl, measure all of the dry ingredients and stir in the milk slowly, to keep the mixture smooth. Add the vanilla.

4. Pour the batter into the pan, directly over the butter. Spread the batter in an even layer.

5. Pit the cherries and scatter them on top of the batter.

6. Place the cobbler in the oven and bake for 40 to 45 minutes, or until the top is a deep golden brown.

7. It is best to serve the cobbler while still warm, since its puffiness disappears as the pie cools. If served cold, cover with sweetened whipped cream.

BOSC PEAR PIE

Elizabeth Schneider Colchie

6 to 8 servings

Pastry:
2½ CUPS ALL-PURPOSE FLOUR
½ TEASPOON SALT
9 TABLESPOONS (1 STICK PLUS 1 TABLESPOON) BUTTER, CHILLED AND CUT INTO TINY BITS
5 TABLESPOONS LARD, CHILLED AND CUT INTO SMALL PIECES
6 TABLESPOONS ICE WATER, AP-PROXIMATELY

Filling:
¼ CUP FINE GINGERSNAP CRUMBS
5 CUPS VERY THINLY SLICED PEARS (ABOUT 7 MEDIUM-SIZED PEARS)

¾ CUP LIGHT BROWN SUGAR
2 TABLESPOONS LEMON JUICE
2 TABLESPOONS POTATO STARCH
1 TABLESPOON VERY FINELY MINCED CANDIED GINGER
1 TEASPOON GRATED LEMON RIND
¼ TEASPOON SALT
1 TABLESPOON BUTTER, CUT INTO BITS
1 EGG
1 TABLESPOON MILK

1. Sift the flour and salt into a bowl.

2. With a pastry blender, cut in the shortenings until the pieces are rice-sized.

3. Sprinkle in the water, a tablespoon at a time, tossing the flour to mix it evenly. When the dough can be massed together easily with the hands, form it into a rough disk, wrap it in plastic and refrigerate for at least 1 hour.

4. Cut off slightly less than half the dough and return it to the refrigerator. Roll out the larger piece and press it into a 9'' pie plate.

5. Sprinkle the pastry with the gingersnap crumbs and refrigerate the shell for about 30 minutes.

6. Meanwhile, in a bowl, combine the pears, sugar, lemon juice, potato starch, ginger, lemon rind, salt and butter. Stir and let the mixture stand about 30 minutes.

7. Preheat the oven to 450 F.

8. Pour the filling into the shell.

9. Roll out the remaining disk of refrigerated pastry to form an upper crust about 10'' in diameter. Moisten the bottom rim of the pie shell with water and firmly press on the upper crust, molding the edge to form a decorative rim. Cut a small hole in the center of the pie and make several slashes in the top crust.

10. Bake the pie on the lowest rack in the oven for 15 minutes.

11. Make an egg wash by beating the egg with the milk. Brush the pastry lightly and evenly with the egg wash, then reduce the heat to 350 F. and bake for about 50 minutes longer, or until the pastry is nicely browned and crisp and the juices bubble out.

MAPLE WALNUT PIE

Florence Fabricant

8 servings

PASTRY FOR A 9" SINGLE-CRUST PIE
1 CUP WALNUT HALVES
¾ CUP DARK CORN SYRUP
¾ CUP PURE MAPLE SYRUP
4 TABLESPOONS (½ STICK) BUTTER,
  MELTED

3 EGGS, LIGHTLY BEATEN
1 TEASPOON VANILLA EXTRACT
½ CUP CHOPPED WALNUTS
WHIPPED CREAM, VANILLA ICE CREAM
  OR MAPLE WALNUT ICE CREAM
  (OPTIONAL)

1. Preheat the oven to 450 F.

2. Line a 9" pie pan with the pastry, prick it all over and weight it with a piece of foil covered with dry beans or with aluminum pastry weights.

3. Bake for 5 to 8 minutes, until the pastry is dry, but has not colored. Remove the foil, reprick the pastry and bake another 2 minutes.

4. Remove the pastry from the oven and lower the temperature to 350 F. Line the pastry shell with the walnut halves.

5. Combine the remaining ingredients, except the whipped cream or ice cream and pour into the pie shell, disturbing the walnut halves as little as possible. The walnut halves will float to the top and you may position them in an attractive pattern.

6. Bake for 40 minutes.

7. Allow to cool and serve with whipped cream or ice cream.

FUDGE BOTTOM PIE

Paula J. Buchholz

8 servings

1¼ CUPS GRAHAM CRACKER CRUMBS
4 TABLESPOONS (½ STICK) BUTTER,
  SOFTENED
¼ CUP GRANULATED SUGAR
½ TEASPOON GROUND CINNAMON
3 OUNCES UNSWEETENED CHOCOLATE

⅓ CUP CONFECTIONERS' SUGAR
⅓ CUP BOILING WATER
1 PACKAGE (3¾ OUNCES) VANILLA
  PUDDING AND PIE FILLING MIX
2 CUPS MILK
HEAVY CREAM, WHIPPED

1. Preheat the oven to 375 F.

2. Combine the graham cracker crumbs, butter, granulated sugar and cinnamon until well mixed. Pour the crumb mixture into a 9" pie plate and press it firmly against the bottom and sides.

3. Bake the pie crust 8 minutes, then cool.

4. Melt the chocolate. Beat in the confectioners' sugar and boiling water. When

the mixture is smooth and thick, spread it over the bottom of the graham cracker crust.

5. In a saucepan, stir together the pudding mix and milk. Cook over medium heat, stirring, until the mixture comes to a full bubbling boil. Cool about 5 minutes, stirring once or twice, then pour into the graham cracker crust; cool thoroughly.

6. Top with whipped cream just before serving.

CURRANT CHIFFON PIE

Raymond Sokolov

One 9" pie

Crust:
16 GRAHAM CRACKERS, FINELY CRUSHED
1 TEASPOON FLOUR
8 TABLESPOONS (1 STICK) BUTTER, SOFTENED
½ CUP SUGAR
1 TEASPOON CINNAMON

Filling:
1 ENVELOPE (1 TABLESPOON) UN-FLAVORED GELATIN
3 EGGS, SEPARATED
⅓ CUP SUGAR
1 CUP SWEETENED CURRANT JUICE*
1 TABLESPOON LEMON JUICE
¼ TEASPOON SALT
1 CUP HEAVY CREAM

1. Preheat the oven to 375 F.

2. Blend all of the crust ingredients thoroughly. Press evenly and firmly over the bottom and sides of a buttered, 9" pie plate. Bake for 10 minutes. Cool and chill.

3. Soften the gelatin in ¼ cup cold water.

4. Beat the egg yolks with half of the sugar. Add the currant juice, lemon juice and salt.

5. Cook, stirring constantly, over very low heat until the mixture coats a spoon. Add the softened gelatin and stir until dissolved.

6. Cool and then chill until the mixture begins to thicken. Whip until fluffy.

7. Beat the egg whites, adding the remaining sugar gradually, until the mixture holds peaks. Fold into the whipped gelatin mixture.

8. Turn the filling into the chilled pie shell and chill until firm.

9. At serving time, whip the cream until stiff and spread it evenly over the pie or decorate the pie with whipped cream piped through a pastry tube.

* To make 1 cup currant juice, wash 1 quart of fresh berries, crush slightly, and heat with a small amount of water until softened. Strain through a piece of cloth, squeezing it tightly. Sweeten with 2 tablespoons of sugar.

MINCEMEAT TARTS

Rona Deme

2 dozen tarts

This is a recipe my mother used, which she in turn got from *her* mother. On Christmas Eve, it is traditional to leave three or four mince tarts on a plate, with a glass of sherry, for Father Christmas to have when he comes to fill the stockings. The mincemeat must be prepared at least six weeks before making the tarts.

Mincemeat:
¼ POUND BEEF SUET*, SHREDDED
¼ POUND (1 CUP) GRATED APPLE
1 POUND MIXED, DRIED FRUITS
  (RAISINS AND CURRANTS)
¼ POUND BLANCHED ALMONDS
¼ POUND MIXED, *GLACÉED* CITRUS
  PEEL (LEMON AND ORANGE), DICED
¼ POUND (1 CUP) BROWN SUGAR
JUICE AND FINELY GRATED RIND OF
  1 LARGE LEMON
½ TEASPOON CINNAMON
½ TEASPOON FRESHLY GRATED
  NUTMEG
¼ CUP BRANDY

Flaky Pastry:
2 CUPS ALL-PURPOSE FLOUR
PINCH OF SALT
12 TABLESPOONS (1½ STICKS) BUTTER
WATER

Other Ingredients:
1 EGG, BEATEN
GRANULATED SUGAR
CONFECTIONERS' SUGAR

1. Combine all of the ingredients for the mincemeat and mix together thoroughly. Place in a large stoneware crock or three to four pint jars, cover well with waxed paper and store in a cool, dry place for at least six weeks.

   Note: This recipe makes much more than needed for the tarts, but it keeps indefinitely, so it pays to make a large batch at one time. Do not cut down the quantities for fat, sugar or brandy or the mincemeat will not store well. Also, make certain that the fruit is dry. If you wash it, allow it to dry for 24 hours before using.

2. To make the pastry, sift the flour and salt together. Divide the butter into three equal portions and rub one portion (4 tablespoons) into the flour until it is crumbly in texture. Stir in enough cold water to make a rollable dough.

3. Roll the dough into a rectangle. Divide one of the two remaining portions of butter into smaller pieces and dot it over two-thirds of the rectangle. Fold the unbuttered end over the middle third of the rectangle, then fold the opposite buttered end over that.

4. Give the pastry a quarter turn, seal the edges and press a rolling pin crosswise into the surface of the pastry at 1½" to 2" intervals, giving it a ridged appearance. This equalizes the air pockets within the dough and makes it puff more evenly when baked.

5. Roll the dough into a rectangle again and repeat the process with the remaining portion of butter. Refrigerate for 30 minutes.

6. Repeat the rolling, folding, sealing and ridging one more time, for a total of three "turns." Refrigerate again at least 30 minutes before using.

7. Preheat the oven to 400 F.

8. When ready to make the tarts, roll the dough to the thickness of $1/8$'' and cut out as many circles as possible with a $2\frac{1}{2}$''-round cookie cutter. Gather up the scraps and reroll, continuing until you have 48 circles (two circles for each tart).

9. Line shallow $2^3/_8$'' tart tins with half of the pastry circles. Fill each with 1 or 2 teaspoons of the mincemeat and cover with the remaining pastry circles.

10. Prick each with a fork, brush with the beaten egg and sprinkle lightly with granulated sugar.

11. Bake in the preheated oven for 25 minutes, until golden brown.

12. Cool the tarts slightly, then remove them from the tins and cool completely on a wire rack. Store in an airtight tin. Dust with confectioners' sugar before serving. Mincemeat tarts are holiday fare, and are usually served at Christmas and New Years' with a glass of sherry.

* The best suet comes from the outside of a beef kidney. Ask the butcher for it.

PURE STRAWBERRY PIE

Carol Cutler

8 servings

6 CUPS FRESH STRAWBERRIES
5 TABLESPOONS CORNSTARCH
1 CUP SUGAR
2 TABLESPOONS LEMON JUICE
1 TEASPOON ORANGE LIQUEUR
ONE 9" PIE SHELL, BAKED
1 CUP WHIPPING CREAM, WHIPPED
  AND SWEETENED

1. Wash, hull, and dry the strawberries. Reserve about 2 cups of the largest and best-looking berries.

2. Into a heavy pot, put the remaining 4 cups of berries and mash them. Add the cornstarch, sugar and lemon juice. Stir well and put the pot over low to moderate heat. Stir constantly, until the mixture becomes thick and clear.

3. Add the orange liqueur and cook for 1 minute longer. Cool, then chill.

4. At serving time, cut the reserved 2 cups of berries in half, lengthwise, and place them in the bottom of the baked pie shell, cut side down. Reserve a few whole berries to decorate the top, if desired.

5. Spoon the chilled strawberry purée over the berries and smooth the top nicely. Spread the whipped cream over the top of the pie, but leave a large circle in the center exposed. If desired, decorate the pie with the reserved whole berries by placing them in the center.

Note: If the pie must be assembled before serving time, try to limit its standing time to 2 or 3 hours. The juice of the berries will cause the crust to become limp.

Savory and Sweet Turnovers

TURNOVERS STUFFED WITH PEAS AND POTATOES (SAMOSAS)

Satish Sehgal

24 *samosas*

Pastry:
2 CUPS ALL-PURPOSE FLOUR
PINCH OF SALT
4 TABLESPOONS VEGETABLE OIL
5 TABLESPOONS WATER

Filling:
½ POUND POTATOES
2 TABLESPOONS VEGETABLE OIL
1 MEDIUM-SIZED ONION, PEELED
  AND FINELY CHOPPED
ONE 1"-LONG PIECE FRESH GINGER,
  PEELED AND FINELY CHOPPED
2 GREEN CHILES, FINELY CHOPPED

1 CUP FRESH OR FROZEN GREEN
  PEAS
1 TEASPOON SALT
½ TEASPOON CAYENNE PEPPER
¼ CUP WATER
¾ TEASPOON ALLSPICE OR *GARAM
  MASALA* (AVAILABLE IN INDIAN
  MARKETS)
½ TEASPOON GROUND CORIANDER
2 TABLESPOONS LEMON JUICE

Other Ingredients:
FLOUR
VEGETABLE OIL

1. Sift together the flour and salt. With your hand, rub in 3 tablespoons of the oil, until the mixture resembles fine bread crumbs. Add the water and mix to make a smooth dough.

2. Knead the dough for 10 minutes and then form it into a ball. Brush with the remaining tablespoon of oil and cover with a damp cloth. Set aside in a cool place until ready to use.

3. Boil the potatoes in their jackets until just tender, then dip them in cold water. Peel and cut them into very small, neat cubes.

4. In a frying pan, heat the oil and fry the onions. Add the ginger, green chiles, peas, salt and cayenne. Stir and cook for 3 minutes.

5. Add ¼ cup of water and cook over low heat for 15 minutes.

6. Add the boiled, diced potatoes, *garam masala* (or allspice), ground coriander and lemon juice. Stir and cook over medium heat for 4 minutes. Remove from the heat and cool.

7. Divide the dough into 24 equal parts and shape into balls. Dredge them in flour and roll each into a thin, 5"-diameter round.

8. Cut each round in half and moisten the edges of the semicircles formed. Make

a wide cone with each semicircle by bringing the ends of the straight edge together, overlapping the two layers of dough by ¼'' and pressing the seam together.

9. Fill the cone thus formed with a tablespoon of filling. Moisten the inside edges of the curved opening, fold them together over the filling and press shut. Pinch the edge closed and decorate it with very small scallops.

10. Prepare all the *samosas* in this manner, keeping them covered with plastic wrap as you work.

11. Fill a wok or deep fryer with vegetable oil to a depth of 3'' or 4'' and place it over medium heat. When the oil is hot, drop in as many *samosas* as will fit without crowding, and fry until crisp and golden. Remove with a slotted spoon and drain on paper towels.

Note: If the *samosas* brown too quickly, lower the heat. They can be reheated in a 300 F. oven.

12. Arrange on a platter and serve hot with mint chutney or tomato ketchup.

FRIED PEACH PIES

Nan Mabon

4 servings

VEGETABLE SHORTENING
1½ CUPS FLOUR
¼ CUP ICE WATER
1 CAN (8½ OUNCES) SLICED PEACHES,
  DRAINED AND CHOPPED
1 TABLESPOON CHOPPED DRIED
  PEACHES
¼ TEASPOON CORNSTARCH
1 EGG YOLK BEATEN WITH 1 TABLE-
  SPOON WATER

1. In a bowl, combine 2 tablespoons of shortening with the flour, and cut it in with pastry scrapers, a pastry blender or two knives.

   Note: It is essential to use less shortening than is usually called for in a pie crust or the crust will be leaden.

2. When the flour-shortening mixture is granular in texture, mix in the ice water, using a little more if it is too dry. Blend well, then gather into a flat patty. Refrigerate for at least 30 minutes.

3. In a bowl, mix the drained peach slices with the dried peaches and let sit for 30 minutes.

4. Roll out the dough until it is very thin. Cut out four 4'' x 2½'' rectangles, then cut four 3'' x 2'' rectangles.

5. In an electric frying pan or cast-iron skillet, heat enough vegetable shortening to come at least 1'' up the sides of the pan.

Continued from preceding page

6. Add the cornstarch to the peach mixture and blend well.

7. Put about a tablespoon of the peach mixture in the center of each of the four larger dough rectangles. Brush the edges of the dough with the egg-water wash and place a small rectangle on top of each large one. Fold the edges of the lower rectangles over the edges of the upper rectangles and press the edges together with a fork.

8. By this time the oil should register 365 F. Put two of the pies at a time into the hot oil, and hold them down with a spatula so they are completely submerged. When they are crisp and browned, remove and drain them. Repeat with the remaining two pies.

9. Serve immediately while still hot.

BAKED SAVORY CHEESE TURNOVERS

Vilma Liacouras Chantiles

20 turnovers

Filling:
1½ CUPS *FETA* CHEESE, APPROXI-
  MATELY
1 CUP MILK
2 TABLESPOONS BUTTER OR MARGA-
  RINE
2 TABLESPOONS FLOUR
PINCH OF SALT
PINCH OF WHITE PEPPER
3 GRATINGS OF NUTMEG
1 EGG

Dough:
½ CUP FINE VEGETABLE OIL
½ CUP WATER OR MILK
PINCH OF SALT
2¼ TO 2½ CUPS FLOUR,
  APPROXIMATELY
MARGARINE OR OIL FOR GLAZE
  (OPTIONAL)

1. Crumble the *feta* with your fingers or a fork and set aside.

2. In a saucepan, scald the milk and then remove it from the heat.

3. In another saucepan, heat the butter (or margarine) for 1 minute without browning. Stir in the flour and continue stirring over medium heat for 2 minutes. Remove from the heat.

4. Stirring with a whisk, gradually add the scalded milk and whisk until the sauce is smooth.

5. Place the pan over medium heat and cook, stirring, until the sauce boils. Lower the heat and simmer for 3 to 4 minutes, until slightly thickened. Season with the salt, pepper and nutmeg. Cool.

6. Lightly beat the eggs and stir them into the cooled sauce.

7. Combine ¾ cup of the sauce with the *feta*. Add more *feta* or sauce, as necessary, until the mixture is thick enough to mound when dropped from a spoon. Refrigerate until ready to assemble the turnovers.

8. In a large bowl, combine the oil and water (or milk). Add the salt, then begin adding the flour, stirring by hand or machine. Add enough flour to form a soft and pliable dough, then knead for a few minutes. If making the dough in advance, cover and refrigerate it until an hour before rolling.

9. Preheat the oven to 375 F.

10. Dust a surface liberally with flour. If the dough seems oily, work the flour into the dough by kneading for several minutes. Using a rolling pin, roll out one-third of the dough until it is thin enough to see through.

11. Using a glass, lid, or other sharp-edged round object 5'' in diameter (a ravioli cutting wheel works well), cut the dough into circles without lifting them off the work surface.

12. Heap 1 tablespoon of filling near the center of each dough circle. Slip a flat spatula under one side of the circle and flip it up to enclose the filling, forming a half-moon.

13. Align and flute the edges. For a decorative effect, press the tines of a fork between the flutings.

14. Repeat with the remaining two-thirds of the dough.

15. Place the turnovers on a baking sheet and brush them lightly with margarine or oil for a glaze, if desired.

16. Bake the turnovers in the preheated oven for 15 to 18 minutes, until crisp and golden chestnut in color. Serve hot.

FRESH BLACKBERRY TURNOVERS

Paula J. Buchholz   16 servings

Sour Cream Dough:
3 CUPS SIFTED ALL-PURPOSE FLOUR
2 TABLESPOONS SUGAR
PINCH OF SALT
½ POUND (2 STICKS) BUTTER OR
  MARGARINE
1 CUP SOUR CREAM
¼ TEASPOON LEMON JUICE

Blackberry Filling:
1 CAN (15 OUNCES) UNPEELED
  APRICOT HALVES
2 TABLESPOONS CORNSTARCH
4 TABLESPOONS SUGAR
DASH OF GROUND CARDAMOM
DASH OF GROUND NUTMEG
DASH OF GROUND CLOVES
1 QUART (4 CUPS) FRESH BLACK-
  BERRIES

1. Mix together the flour, sugar and salt.

2. With a pastry blender or fork, cut in the butter or margarine until the mixture is crumbly.

3. Add the sour cream and lemon juice and mix until the dough sticks together and forms a ball.

4. On a lightly floured board, knead until the dough is smooth and elastic.

5. Wrap the dough in waxed paper and chill several hours, or, even better, overnight.

Continued from preceding page

6. Divide the dough in half. Keep one half of the chilled dough in the refrigerator until you are ready to use it. Roll out the other half—from the center to the edges—until it measures a rectangle 16'' x 10''.

7. Fold the dough in thirds. Give it a quarter turn, roll out again and fold into thirds again. Repeat this rolling and folding process until the dough has been rolled out and folded four times. Wrap the dough tightly and return it to the refrigerator.

8. Roll and fold the other half of the dough in the same manner.

9. Next, prepare the filling. Drain the liquid from the apricots into a measuring cup. Add enough water to the liquid to measure 1 cup. Reserve the apricots.

10. In a medium-sized saucepan, combine the apricot liquid with the cornstarch, sugar, cardamom, nutmeg and cloves. Then stir in the blackberries.

11. Bring the mixture to a boil, stirring constantly. Boil 1 minute, then remove the saucepan from the heat and stir in the apricots; cool.

12. When ready to fill the turnovers, preheat the oven to 400 F.

13. Remove half of the pastry dough from the refrigerator and roll it out into a 20'' x 10'' rectangle. Cut the rectangle into eight 5'' squares.

14. Place about 2 tablespoons of filling in the center of each pastry square. Fold the pastry over diagonally to form a triangle. Crimp the edges of the pastry triangle with a fork, so the turnover is tightly sealed.

15. Place the turnovers on an ungreased baking sheet. Brush the top of each with water and then sprinkle lightly with granulated sugar. Just before baking, cut a small slash in the top of each turnover to allow any steam to escape.

16. Lower the oven temperature to 375 F. as soon as you put in the turnovers. Bake about 25 minutes, until the turnovers are puffed and browned.

CORNISH PASTIES

Rona Deme

12 pasties

Puff Pastry:
2 CUPS (8 OUNCES) ALL-PURPOSE
  FLOUR
GOOD PINCH OF SALT
SEVERAL DROPS OF LEMON JUICE
½ POUND (2 STICKS) BUTTER

1 MEDIUM-SIZED ONION, FINELY
  CHOPPED
¼ CUP COLD WATER
½ TEASPOON SALT
¼ TEASPOON PEPPER
1 EGG, BEATEN

Filling:
1 POUND GROUND BEEF
½ POUND COOKED, PEELED POTA-
  TOES, MASHED*

1. Sift the flour and salt together, then mix with the lemon juice and enough water to form a workable, rollable dough.

2. Roll the dough out to form a rectangle about 8'' x 16''. Place the butter cross-wise across the center and fold first one short end and then the other over the butter, enclosing it completely. Pinch the edges together and turn the pastry at a right angle, so that a short edge faces you. Press a rolling pin into the surface of the pastry at regular intervals, giving it a ribbed appearance. This helps to distribute the air evenly inside the pastry "package," which will make it rise more evenly when baked.

3. Again roll the dough into a rectangle, fold the bottom third over the center third, then fold the top third over the bottom third, forming three layers. Seal the edges, turn, and press with the rolling pin.

4. Repeat this process five more times, for a total of seven "turns."

   Note: It will be necessary to allow the pastry to rest in the refrigerator once or twice between rollings, to prevent it from becoming too soft and sticky.

5. After the last turn, allow the dough to rest in the refrigerator for 30 to 60 minutes.

6. Roll the chilled pastry into a sheet about 12'' x 16'' and the thickness of a penny. Using a very sharp knife, cut it into twelve 4'' squares. Put the squares back into the refrigerator for 30 to 60 minutes.

7. Preheat the oven to 475 F.

8. Combine all of the filling ingredients and mix well.

9. Divide the filling mixture into 12 equal portions and place one portion in the center of each pastry square.

10. Brush the edges of the pastry with beaten egg and fold each diagonally to form a triangle. Carefully, but firmly, press the edges together (do not squash the cut edges, or they will not puff properly). Prick the top of each pastry once or twice with a sharp knife and brush with egg.

11. Place the pasties on an ungreased baking sheet and bake for 10 minutes in the preheated oven. Then turn the temperature down to 400 F. and continue baking 15 minutes longer, until the pasties are nice and brown.

* The potatoes are simply cooked and mashed, with no additions. Sometimes I mash them more coarsely, which gives the filling a rougher texture. Add several more tablespoons of water if you do this.

PERUVIAN MEAT TURNOVERS
(EMPANADAS DE PICADILLO PERUANA)

Jeanne Lesem

6 servings

Virtually every Latin American country has its own version of *empanadas*. Most are mildly spiced, compared with the Mexican variety that are most familiar in the United States. Many contain raisins and/or nuts, unpitted olives and sliced, hard-cooked egg.

Continued from preceding page

Crust:
2 CUPS ALL-PURPOSE FLOUR
1 TEASPOON CONFECTIONERS' SUGAR
½ TEASPOON SALT, IF USING HOME-
  MADE STOCK; OMIT IF USING
  CANNED SOUP OR BOUILLON CUBES
½ CUP HOT BEEF STOCK OR
  BOUILLON

Filling:
1 POUND LEAN GROUND BEEF OR
  PORK, OR A MIXTURE OF THE TWO
1 SMALL CAN JALAPEÑO PEPPERS,
  DRAINED, SEEDED AND CHOPPED,
  OR 1 RAW HOT PEPPER, ABOUT
  4" LONG, SEEDED, DERIBBED AND
  FINELY CHOPPED

1 MEDIUM-SIZED ONION, FINELY
  CHOPPED
18 PIMIENTO-STUFFED OLIVES
3 TABLESPOONS RAISINS
¼ CUP CHOPPED FRESH PARSLEY
1 TEASPOON DRIED OREGANO
1 LARGE HARD-COOKED EGG, SLICED
OIL OR RENDERED CHICKEN FAT

1. Measure the flour by lightly spooning it into a measuring cup and leveling the top with the cutting edge of a knife blade. Place the flour on a pastry board or countertop and stir in the sugar and salt (if using).

2. Make a well in the center and add the hot soup all at once. With the fingers of one hand, mix the dough by pushing the flour little by little into the liquid. Then knead the dough until it is smooth and rubbery. Cover with plastic wrap and let stand at room temperature 30 to 60 minutes while preparing the filling.

3. In a lightly greased or non-stick skillet, over medium heat, cook and stir the meat, using a spoon to break up the lumps. When the meat begins to lose its reddish color, add the peppers, onion, olives, raisins, parsley and oregano and cook, stirring occasionally, 20 to 25 minutes. Set aside, uncovered, to cool while you roll the dough.

4. Divide the dough into six equal portions. Keep the remainder covered while you roll and fill each *empanada*. Roll the dough into a circle a scant ⅛" thick. Place one-sixth of the filling toward one side, top with a slice of egg, and paint the outer rim of the dough lightly with water, using a pastry brush or piece of paper towel. Fold the dough circle in half and pinch the edges together to seal tightly. Use fork tines to make a pattern on the edges. Repeat until all the ingredients are used.

5. At this point, you can refrigerate the turnovers in a single layer until time to cook them; or, chill them, then freeze in a single layer and, finally, pack and seal them in freezer bags.

6. To cook, paint all sides with cooking oil or rendered chicken fat, and bake 25 minutes at 350 F. Brush with the pan drippings (or with additional oil or fat), raise the oven temperature to 400 F., and bake 10 minutes longer, or until the crust is lightly browned.

7. Serve hot or at room temperature.